A Comprehensive

Renal Diet Food List Guide

Renal Diet Food List Reference

for Kidney Disease

by Janeth Kingston, BSN RN

Introduction

About This Book

Purpose and Scope

This book aims to provide comprehensive guidance on managing kidney disease through diet. Our goal is to cover a broad range of dietary options suitable for various stages of kidney disease while ensuring the information is evidence-based and practical for everyday use.

The food items in this book have been carefully selected from DA's food database and other reputable scientific sources. This ensures that all dietary recommendations are grounded in the latest nutritional research and clinical guidelines for kidney health.

How to Use This Book

This book is designed to be a user-friendly guide for anyone looking to manage kidney disease through diet. Each section is organized to help you easily find the information you need, whether you're looking for specific foods to include or avoid, meal planning tips, or detailed recipes.

We have categorized foods to make it simple for you to identify kidney-friendly options. The comprehensive food lists are backed by scientific research, not AI-generated, with countless hours poured by our team of dietitians and nurses, providing a reliable resource for making dietary choices that support kidney health.

In addition to the food lists, you'll find practical meal plans and recipes tailored to different stages of kidney disease, ensuring that you can maintain a balanced diet that meets your nutritional needs.

Use the detailed index to quickly locate specific topics or foods. The glossary will help you understand any unfamiliar terms, and the appendices offer additional resources to further support your dietary management.

Chapter 1
Understanding Kidney Disease

In my book "Avoid Dialysis Diet Plan for Kidney Disease", I have extensively outlined the role of diet in Kidney Disease progression but more so in its management. But before we go to the nitty-gritty of this book, let's quickly recap what we are dealing with, how we got to this point, and the primary reason why you are reading this book. *(But feel free to proceed to the next chapter if you think that you already are well equipped with the basics of CKD)*

So, I gotta ask, What is Kidney Disease?

Kidney disease means that the kidneys are damaged and can't filter blood like they should. This damage can cause wastes to build up in the body. It can also cause other problems that can harm your health.

For most people, kidney damage occurs slowly over many years, often due to diabetes or high blood pressure. This is called chronic kidney disease. When someone has a sudden change in kidney function because of illness, or injury, or some medications, this is called acute kidney injury. This can occur in a person with normal kidney function or in someone who already has kidney problems and may be reversible.

Kidney disease is a growing problem. More than 37 million Americans may have kidney disease and many more are at risk. Anyone can develop kidney disease, regardless of age or race. The main risk factors for developing kidney disease are:

- Diabetes,
- High blood pressure,
- Cardiovascular (heart and blood vessel) disease
- A family history of kidney failure
- Poor lifestyle and diet choices

Diagnosis and Symptoms: What are causes of Kidney disease?

Diabetes and high blood pressure are by far the most common causes of kidney disease in the United States. These conditions can slowly damage the kidneys over many years.

Other causes of kidney disease include diseases caused by an individual's immune system fighting the kidney tissue slowly such as in Lupus nephritis.

Sometimes the reason for the kidney disease is not explained and your nephrologist may ask to undergo a kidney biopsy to obtain more information regarding the cause of the kidney disease.

Early kidney disease has no signs or symptoms

- You may not feel any different until your kidney disease is very advanced.
- Blood and urine tests are the only way to know if you have kidney disease.
- A blood test checks your glomerular filtration rate (GFR), which tells how well your kidneys are filtering.
- A urine test checks for protein in your urine.

Kidney disease can be treated or controlled if detected early

- The sooner you know you have kidney disease, the sooner you can get treatment to help delay or prevent kidney failure.
- Treatment may include taking medicines called ACE inhibitors or ARBs to manage high blood pressure and keep your kidneys healthier longer.
- Treating kidney disease may also help prevent heart disease.

Kidney disease usually does not go away

- Instead, it may get worse over time and can lead to kidney failure.
- If the kidneys fail, treatment with dialysis or a kidney transplant is necessary.
- Kidney disease can also lead to other health conditions including heart disease.
- In fact, people with kidney disease are more likely to have a stroke or heart attack.

Monitoring Your Kidney Health

Many people with kidney disease don't have symptoms until their kidney damage is very advanced. For most people, the only way to know about your kidney health is through blood and urine tests. The blood test checks your Glomerular Filtration Rate (GFR) and the urine test checks for albumin. These two tests are also used to follow the progression of your kidney disease.

Know your GFR and urine test results. Keep track of them over time to see how your kidneys are doing. Kidney disease tends to get worse over time. Each time you get checked, ask how the results compare to the last results. The key tests to track kidney health include:

Blood pressure

The most important thing you can do to slow down kidney disease is keep your blood pressure at or below the target set by your health care provider. This may delay or prevent kidney failure.

GFR

The GFR tells you how well your kidneys are filtering blood. GFR stands for glomerular filtration rate. You can't raise your GFR. The goal is to keep your GFR from going down to prevent or delay kidney failure.

STAGES OF CHRONIC KIDNEY DISEASE		GFR*	% OF KIDNEY FUNCTION
Stage 1	Kidney damage with **normal** kidney function	90 or higher	**90-100%**
Stage 2	Kidney damage with **mild loss** of kidney function	89 to 60	**60-89%**
Stage 3a	**Mild to moderate** loss of kidney function	59 to 45	**45-59%**
Stage 3b	**Moderate to severe** loss of kidney function	44 to 30	**30-44%**
Stage 4	**Severe** loss of kidney function	29 to 15	**15-29%**
Stage 5	Kidney **failure**	less than 15	**<15%**

* Your GFR number tells you how much kidney function you have left. As the kidney disease progresses, the GFR number goes down so does your kidney function.

6

Urine albumin

Albumin is a protein in your blood that can pass into the urine when kidneys are damaged. You can't undo kidney damage, but you may be able to lower the amount of albumin in your urine with treatment. Lowering your urine albumin is good for your kidneys.

A1C

For people with diabetes: A1C test is a test that shows the average blood glucose level over the last 3 months. Lowering your A1C can help you to stay healthy.

Now here's something that I can't help but overemphasize when we talk of the role of Renal Diet Foods in Managing Kidney Disease:

Scientific consensus underscores that dietary modifications can significantly affect Chronic Kidney Disease (CKD) progression. Optimal nutrition—emphasizing a low-protein, low-sodium, and high-fiber diet—has been shown to decelerate kidney function decline. Such dietary shifts not only support kidney health, but also mitigate associated risks like hypertension and diabetes. Therefore, bridging the knowledge gap in dietary management is critical for improving CKD outcomes.

Chapter 2
The Basics of a
Kidney-Friendly Diet

Key Nutrients to Monitor: Potassium, Phosphorus, Sodium, and Protein

You may have heard this over and over again but sometimes find it difficult to follow through because valuable information is just inundating. I wish there was a shortcut to knowing all this information, but I have created this chapter into seemingly bite-sized nuggets that you can churn out into something actionable and helpful for your CKD diet management.

What Should You Eat for Your CKD?

As always, it is important to follow a healthy diet for CKD to maintain good nutritional status and slow its progression. Consider the following as steps in following through proper diet and nutrition while paying particular attention to the 4 key nutrients that we need to monitor for your kidney health.

1. Follow a low-sodium diet and read labels.

- To keep your blood pressure below 130/80 mmHg
- Daily sodium intake should be less than 2000 –2300mg
- Purchase more fresh foods and low-sodium frozen foods.
- Use herbs instead of regular seasonings.
- Read nutrition fact labels on all foods: choose sodium-free, salt-free, very low sodium, light, or reduced-sodium items instead of regular foods

2. Eat an appropriate amount of protein for your need

- Eat small portions of protein foods: meat, poultry, fish, eggs, dairy products, and beans.
- Ask your dietitian how much protein you need per day.
- Do not follow commercial weight reduction diets such as South Beach, and low carbohydrate diets.

Animal Protein Source	Plant Protein Source
Chicken, fish, beef, pork, lamb, eggs, dairy products	Beans, nuts, lentils, tofu, grains

3. Use healthy cooking

- Grill, broil, bake, roast, or stir-fry foods and avoid deep frying.
- Trim fat from meat and remove skin from poultry
- Use non-stick margarine or oil instead of butter and choose low-fat products

Heart-healthy foods
Lean cuts of meat (loin or round), poultry without skin, fish, beans, vegetables, fruits, and low-fat milk, yogurt, cheese

4. Choose foods with an adequate amount of potassium

- You may need low potassium with the progression of CKD and taking medication as prescribed by your physician like ACEI or ARB (Lisinopril, or Avapro)
- Limit high-potassium foods
- Avoid lite salt because it is made of potassium instead of sodium
- Do not drink or use the liquid from canned fruits or vegetables
- Remember portion size!!!

High Potassium Foods	Low Potassium Foods
Potatoes (white and sweet), tomatoes/tomato products, banana, orange juice, beans, nuts, prune, or prune juice, beans, Milk and dairy products, peanut butter	Apples, peaches, green beans, cauliflower, onion, celery, white bread, pasta, noodles, rice, corn flakes, rice cereal, and rice milk.

5. Choose foods with an adequate amount of phosphorus
   - When your kidney function slows down, you may need to follow a low-phosphorus diet to protect your bone and blood vessels.
   - Limit dairy products, beans, lentils, nuts, organ meats, and dark colas.
   - Watch for "PHOS" on the ingredient list of labels: many packaged foods have phosphorus addition
   - Avoid deli meats that contain phosphorus but consume fresh meats

High Phosphorus Foods	Low Phosphorus Foods
Organ meat, dairy products, beans, lentils, nuts, cola, bran cereals and oatmeal	Fresh fruits and vegetables, breads, pasta, rice milk, corn and rice cereals, light color soda

Hydration and Fluid Management

As we know Chronic Kidney Disease (CKD) is typically categorized into five stages, with Stage 1 being the mildest and Stage 5 being the most severe (often requiring dialysis or a kidney transplant). It's important to note that fluid intake recommendations can, vary widely based on individual circumstances, including the patient's size, activity level, climate, and presence of other health conditions. Therefore, these should be considered general guidelines and actual fluid needs should be determined in consultation with your healthcare provider.

Here are some general guidelines based on the stages of CKD:

Stage 1 (Kidney damage with normal or increased GFR, GFR ≥90 mL/min): At this stage, there may not be any specific restrictions on fluid intake unless other health conditions warrant it. The usual recommendation for healthy adults applies, which is typically around 2 to 2.5 liters per day or 8-10 glasses of water. However, overconsumption should be avoided.

Stage 2 (Kidney damage with mildly decreased GFR, GFR 60-89 mL/min): Similarly to Stage 1, there may not be any specific fluid restrictions unless warranted by other health conditions. Maintaining adequate hydration is still important.

Stage 3 (Moderate decrease in GFR, GFR 30-59 mL/min): As kidney function declines further, patients may start to experience fluid retention leading to swelling and high blood pressure. In this case, a healthcare provider may recommend limiting fluid intake.

Stage 4 (Severe reduction in GFR, GFR 15-29 mL/min): At this stage, the kidneys have lost a significant amount of their filtering capabilities. Fluid restrictions are more likely at this stage to prevent fluid overload.

Stage 5 (Kidney failure, GFR <15 mL/min or on dialysis): Fluid intake is usually strictly controlled at this stage, especially for patients on dialysis. The amount of fluid a patient can have is often based on their urine output and the amount of fluid removed during dialysis. It's common for patients on hemodialysis to be advised to limit their fluid intake to 1-1.5 liters per day.

Again, these are general guidelines and individual recommendations can vary widely. It's important for patients to work closely with their healthcare provider to determine the appropriate fluid intake for their specific circumstances.

Chapter 3
The Renal Diet
Food List

Welcome to the heart of this book. As I have mentioned earlier, the data contained in this food list had been properly curated with a team of dietitians and nephrology nurses pouring countless hours in coming up with this list and gathering scientific data from the USDA Food Data Central and other scientific sources, making the data accurate and reliable to be used as a reference for your CKD diet management as prescribed by your physician and dietitian. Additionally, you may find an index on Appendix C (page 175) of this book to make it easier for you to locate the specific food you are looking for.

How to use the charts

1. The charts are categorized into general food groups: Carbohydrates, Fats (oils, nuts, and seeds), Milk, Fruits & Vegetables, Vegetable Proteins, Meats, Poultry, & Seafoods, Herbs & Spices

2. Locate your specific food through the Categories, alternatively through the indices available on Appendix C (page 175).

3. Each specific food groups are further categorized into their preparations which have the standardized amount of 100 grams. Measurements such as slices, tsps., tbsps. or cups are available below the 100 grams standardized measurement with their corresponding specific amount in grams.

4. Per 100 grams of the specific food type, you will find its corresponding amount of nutrients: Calories, Carbs, Proteins, Fats, Sodium, Phosphorus, and Potassium.

5. You may then divide or multiply it by the amount of food that you are preparing in your recipe to get the actual nutrient content.

Example 1: Actual Nutrient Content in Your Recipe

The recipe calls for 1 cup of boiled asparagus. Based on the food list chart, you will need to multiply the amount of nutrients by 2, since 90 grams of boiled asparagus is only ½ of a cup (or 0.50 cup).

ASPARAGUS	SERVING QUANTITY	SERVING UNIT	CALORIES (kCal)	PROTEIN (g)	TOTAL CARBOHYDRATES (g)	SODIUM (mg)	POTASSIUM (mg)	PHOSPHORUS (mg)	TOTAL FAT (g)
boiled,	100.00	g	22	2.4	4.1	14.00	224.00	54.00	0.22
drained	90.00	g	20	2.2	3.7	12.60	201.60	48.60	0.20
	0.50	c							

For this specific example, the nutrient content of 1 cup of asparagus will now be:

Calories:	40 kCal
Protein:	4.4 g
Carbs:	7.4 g
Fats:	0.40g
Sodium:	25.2 g
Potassium:	403 g ↑
Phosphorus:	97.2 g

Example 2: More on Reading and Using the chart
6 pieces of frozen Asparagus is approximately 87 grams. So you base

ASPARAGUS	SERVING QUANTITY	SERVING UNIT	CALORIES (kCal)	PROTEIN (g)	TOTAL CARBOHYDRATES (g)	SODIUM (mg)	POTASSIUM (mg)	PHOSPHORUS (mg)	TOTAL FAT (g)
boiled,	100.00	g	22	2.4	4.1	14.00	224.00	54.00	0.22
drained	90.00	g	20	2.2	3.7	12.60	201.60	48.60	0.20
	0.50	c							
frozen	100.00	g	24	3.2	4.1	8.00	253.00	64.00	0.23
	87.00	g	21	2.8	3.6	6.96	220.11	55.68	0.20
	6.00	pcs							

your nutrients on the 87grams line. If you wish to reduce your potassium intake, you may opt to eat only 3 pieces which will lower the potassium from 220.11 to approximately 110mg only.

Alternatively, you may want to use a scale, measure your food, and base your reduction or addition on the 100 grams mark depending on your daily needs and restrictions.

13

A. Vegetables

Hey there!

Do you need to print out this Food List?

You can download a printable version of this chart by scanning the QR code below or copying the link on your computer browser.

https://go.renaltracker.com/printfoodlist

Vegetables

ASPARAGUS	SERVING QUANTITY	SERVING UNIT	CALORIES (kCal)	PROTEIN (g)	TOTAL CARBOHYDRATES (g)	SODIUM (mg)	POTASSIUM (mg)	PHOSPHORUS (mg)	TOTAL FAT (g)
boiled,	100.00	g	22	2.4	4.1	14.00	224.00	54.00	0.22
drained	90.00	g	20	2.2	3.7	12.60	201.60	48.60	0.20
	0.50	c							
frozen	100.00	g	24	3.2	4.1	8.00	253.00	64.00	0.23
	87.00	g	21	2.8	3.6	6.96	220.11	55.68	0.20
	6.00	pcs							
frozen,	100.00	g	18	3.0	1.9	3.00	172.00	49.00	0.42
boiled, drained	90.00	g	16	2.7	1.7	2.70	154.80	44.10	0.38
	0.50	c							
canned,	100.00	g	19	2.1	2.5	287.00	172.00	43.00	0.65
drained	121.00	g	23	2.6	3.0	347.27	208.12	52.03	0.79
	0.50	c							
BEANS									
green wax,	100.00	g	31	1.8	7.0	6.00	211.00	38.00	
raw	82.50	g	26	1.5	5.8	4.95	174.08	31.35	
	0.75	c							
green wax,	100.00	g	33	1.8	7.5	3.00	186.00	32.00	
frozen	82.67	g	27	1.5	6.2	2.48	153.76	26.45	
	0.67	c							
green wax,	100.00	g	35	1.9	7.9	1.00	146.00	29.00	
boiled,	125.00	g	44	2.4	9.9	1.25	182.50	36.25	
drained	1.00	c							
green wax,	100.00	g	21	1.1	4.2	268.00	96.00	22.00	
canned,	135.00	g	28	1.4	5.7	361.80	129.60	29.70	
drained	1.00	c							
CARROTS									
strips, slices	100.00	g	41	0.9	9.6	69.00	320.00	35.00	
	122.00	g	50	1.1	11.7	84.18	390.40	42.70	
	1.00	c							
grated	100.00	g	41	0.9	9.6	69.00	320.00	35.00	
	82.50	g	34	0.8	7.9	56.93	264.00	28.88	
	0.75	c							
sliced, boiled	100.00	g	35	0.8	8.2	58.00	235.00	30.00	
drained, no	78.00	g	27	0.6	6.4	45.24	183.30	23.40	
salt	0.50	c							
frozen	100.00	g	36	0.8	7.9	68.00	235.00	33.00	
	85.33	g	31	0.7	6.7	58.03	200.53	28.16	
	0.67	c							
baby	100.00	g	35	0.6	8.2	78.00	237.00	28.00	
	80.00	g	28	0.5	6.6	62.40	189.60	22.40	
	8.00	pcs							
juice,	100.00	g	40	1.0	9.3	66.00	292.00	42.00	
canned	236.00	g	94	2.2	21.9	155.76	689.12	99.12	
	8.00	fl oz							

15

TOMATO	SERVING QUANTITY	SERVING UNIT	CALORIES (kCal)	PROTEIN (g)	TOTAL CARBOHYDRATES (g)	SODIUM (mg)	POTASSIUM (mg)	PHOSPHORUS (mg)	TOTAL FAT (g)
red, whole	100.00	g	18	0.9	3.9	5.00	237	24.00	
medium 2.6 in	123.00	g	22	1.1	4.8	6.15	292	29.52	
diameter	1.00	pc							
diced or	100.00	g	18	0.9	3.9	5.00	237	24.00	
chopped	90.00	g	16	0.8	3.5	4.50	213	21.60	
	0.50	c							
yellow,	100.00	g	15	1.0	3.0	23.00	258	36.00	
chopped	92.67	g	14	0.9	2.8	21.31	239	33.36	
	0.67	c							
orange,	100.00	g	16	1.2	3.2	42.00	212	29.00	
chopped	79.00	g	13	0.9	2.5	33.18	167	22.91	
	0.50	c							
green	100.00	g	23	1.2	5.1	13.00	204	28.00	
	90.00	g	21	1.1	4.6	11.70	183	25.20	
	0.50	c							
whole, canned	100.00	g	16	0.8	3.5	115	191	17.00	
	240.00	g	38	1.9	8.3	276	458	40.80	
	1.00	c							
sauce, canned,	100.00	g	24	1.2	5.3	11.00	297	27.00	
no salt	244.00	g	59	2.9	13.0	26.84	725	65.88	
	1.00	c							
crushed,	100.00	g	32	1.6	7.3	186	293	32.00	
canned	56.70	g	18	0.9	4.1	106	166	18.14	
	2.00	oz							
paste, canned	100.00	g	82	4.3	18.9	790	1,014	83.00	
	32.80	g	27	1.4	6.2	259	333	27.22	
	2.00	tbsp							
puree, canned,	100.00	g	38	1.7	9.0	28.00	439	40.00	
no salt	250.00	g	95	4.1	22.5	70.00	1,098	100.00	
	1.00	c							
sun dried, in	100.00	g	213	5.1	23.3	266	1,565	139.00	
oil, drained	27.50	g	59	1.4	6.4	73.15	430	38.23	
	0.25	c							
Ketchup, low	100.00	g	101	1.0	27.4	20.00	281	26.00	
sodium	15.00	g	15	0.2	4.1	3.00	42.15	3.90	
	1.00	tbsp							
juice, canned	100.00	g	17	0.9	3.5	253	217	19.00	
	243.00	g	41	2.1	8.6	614	527	46.17	
	8.00	fl oz							
cherry, sweet,	100.00	g	63	1.1	16.0	0.00	222	21.00	
raw	138.00	g	87	1.5	22.1	0.00	306	29.00	
	1.00	c							

PEPPER

PEPPER	SERVING QUANTITY	SERVING UNIT	CALORIES (kCal)	PROTEIN (g)	TOTAL CARBOHYDRATES (g)	SODIUM (mg)	POTASSIUM (mg)	PHOSPHORUS (mg)	TOTAL FAT (g)
bell, sweet yellow, 3 in diameter	100.00	g	27	1.0	6.3	2.00	212.00	24.00	
	186.00	g	50	1.9	11.8	3.72	394.32	44.64	
	1.00	pc							
bell, sweet green, chopped	100.00	g	20	0.9	4.6	3.00	175.00	20.00	
	74.50	g	15	0.6	3.5	2.24	130.38	14.90	
	0.50	c							
bell, sweet green, sauteed	100.00	g	116	0.8	4.2	17.00	134.00	15.00	
bell, sweet red, chopped	100.00	g	26	1.0	6.0	4.00	211.00	26.00	
	74.50	g	19	0.7	4.5	2.98	157.20	19.37	
	0.50	c							
bell, sweet red, sauteed	100.00	g	133	1.0	6.6	21.00	193.00	23.00	
bell, sweet red, chopped, frozen, drained, boiled, no salt added	100.00	g	16	1.0	3.3	4.00	72.00	13.00	
	85.05	g	14	0.8	2.8	3.40	61.24	11.06	
	3.00	oz							
jalapeno, sliced	100.00	g	29	0.9	6.5	3.00	248.00	26.00	
	22.50	g	7	0.2	1.5	0.68	55.80	5.85	
	0.13	c							
serrano, chopped	100.00	g	32	1.7	6.7	10.00	305.00	40.00	
	26.25	g	8	0.5	1.8	2.63	80.06	10.50	
	0.25	c							
black, ground	100.00	g	251	10.4	64.0	20.00	1,329.00	158.00	
	2.10	g	5	0.2	1.3	0.42	27.91	3.32	
	1.00	tsp							
white, ground	100.00	g	296	10.4	68.6	5.00	73.00	176.00	
	2.40	g	7	0.3	1.7	0.12	1.75	4.22	
	1.00	tsp							
hot chilli, red	100.00	g	40	1.9	8.8	9.00	322.00	43.00	
	45.00	g	18	0.8	4.0	4.05	144.90	19.35	
	1.00	pc							

CABBAGE	SERVING QUANTITY	SERVING UNIT	CALORIES (kcal)	PROTEIN (g)	TOTAL CARBOHYDRATES (g)	SODIUM (mg)	POTASSIUM (mg)	PHOSPHORUS (mg)	TOTAL FAT (g)
green, chopped	100.00	g	25	1.3	5.8	18.00	170.00	26.00	
	89.00	g	22	1.1	5.2	16.02	151.30	23.14	
	1.00	c							
green shredded, sliced	100.00	g	25	1.3	5.8	18.00	170.00	26.00	
	87.50	g	22	1.1	5.1	15.75	148.75	22.75	
	1.25	c							
green, shredded, boiled, drained, no salt added	100.00	g	23	1.3	5.5	8.00	196.00	33.00	
	75.00	g	17	1.0	4.1	6.00	147.00	24.75	
	0.50	c							
chinese, shredded, raw	100.00	g							
	76.00	g	12	0.9		6.84	181.00	22.04	
	1.00	c							
chinese, cooked, no salt	100.00	g							
	75.00	g	17	1.0		6.00	147.00	24.75	
	0.50	c							
red, shredded	100.00	g	31	1.4	7.4	27.00	243.00	30.00	
	87.50	g	27	1.3	6.5	23.63	212.63	26.25	
	1.25	c							
red, shredded, boiled, drained, no salt added	100.00	g	29	1.5	6.9	28.00	262.00	33.00	
	75.00	g	27	1.1	5.2	21.00	196.50	24.75	
	0.50	c							
Bok Choy or White Mustard, shredded	100.00	g	13	1.5	2.2	65.00	252.00	37.00	
	87.50	g	11	1.3	1.9	56.88	220.50	32.38	
	1.25	c							
Bok Choy/ Pak Choi, shredded, boiled, drained	100.00	g	12	1.6	1.8	34.00	371.00	29.00	
	85.00	g	10	1.3	1.5	28.90	315.35	24.65	
	0.50	c							
Kimchi	100.00	g	15	1.1	2.4	498.00	151.00	24.00	
	150.00	g	23	1.7	3.6	747.00	226.50	36.00	
	1.00	c							

MUSH ROOM	SERVING QUANTITY	SERVING UNIT	CALORIES (kCal)	PROTEIN (g)	TOTAL CARBOHYDRATES (g)	SODIUM (mg)	POTASSIUM (mg)	PHOSPHORUS (mg)	TOTAL FAT (g)
Shitake, raw	100.00	g	34	2.2	6.8	9.00	304	112.00	
	19.00	g	6	0.4	1.3	1.71	57.76	21.28	
	1.00	pc							
Shitake, dried	100.00	g	296	9.6	75.4	13.00	1,534	294.00	
	32.40	g	96	3.1	24.4	4.21	497	95.26	
	9.00	pcs							
Shitake, cooked	100.00	g	56	1.6	14.4	4.00	117	29.00	
	72.50	g	41	1.1	10.4	2.90	84.83	21.03	
	0.50	c							
Shitake, stir fried	100.00	g	39	3.5	7.7	5.00	326	111.00	
	108.00	g	42	3.7	8.3	5.40	352	119.88	
	1.00	c							
Portabella/ Portabello	100.00	9	22	2.1	3.9	9.00	364	108.00	
Portabello, grilled	100.00	g	29	3.3	4.4	11.00	437	135.00	
White, raw	100.00	g	22	3.0	3.3	5.00	318	86.00	
	96.00	g	21	3.0	3.1	4.80	305	82.56	
	1.00	c							
white, sliced, stir-fried	100.00	g	26	3.6	4.0	12.00	396	105.00	
	108.00	g	28	3.9	4.4	12.96	428	113.40	
	1.00	c							

LETTUCE									
romaine, shredded	100.00	g	17	1.2	3.3		8.00	247.00	30.00
	70.50	g	12	0.9	2.3		5.64	174.14	21.15
	1.50	c							
butterhead, medium leaves	100.00	g	13	1.4	2.2		5.00	238.00	33.00
	82.50	g	11	1.1	1.8		4.13	196.35	27.23
	11.00	pcs							
Red Leaf, shredded	100.00	g	13	1.3	2.3		25	187	28.00
	28.00	g	4	0.4	0.6		7	52.36	7.84
	1.00	c							
Iceberg, shredded or chopped	100.00	g	14	0.9	3.0		10	141	20.00
	108.00	g	15	1.0	3.2		11	152.28	21.60
	1.50	c							
Iceberg, loose leaves, medium	100.00	g	14	0.9	3.0		10	141.00	20.00
	80.00	g	11	0.7	2.4		8	112.80	16.00
	10.00	pcs							

CORN

	SERVING QUANTITY	SERVING UNIT	CALORIES (kCal)	PROTEIN (g)	TOTAL CARBOHYDRATES (g)	SODIUM (mg)	POTASSIUM (mg)	PHOSPHORUS (mg)	TOTAL FAT (g)
white, sweet	100.00	g	390	7.8	86.6	956.00	88.00	39.00	
	25.00	g	98	2.0	21.7	239.00	22.00	9.75	
	1.00	c							
white, steamed (Navajo)	100.00	g	386	9.7	75.2	4.00	532.00	312.00	
	85.05	g	328	8.3	64.0	3.40	452.47	265.36	
	3.00	oz							
white, stew, steamed (Navajo)	100.00	g	112	8.8	10.8	104.00	177.00	107.00	
	85.05	g	95	7.5	9.2	88.45	150.54	91.00	
	3.00	oz							
sweet, boiled, drained	100.00	g	94	3.1	22.3	4.00	251.00	75.00	0.74
	82.00	g	77	2.6	18.3	3.28	205.82	61.50	0.61
	0.50	c							
flour, white, whole grain	100.00	g	361	6.9	76.9	5.00	315.00	272.00	3.86
	29.25	g	106	2.0	22.5	1.46	92.14	79.56	1.13
	0.25	c							
yellow, sweet, boiled, drained	100.00	g	96	3.4	21.0	1.00	218.00	77.00	1.50
	82.00	g	79	2.8	17.2	0.82	178.76	63.14	1.23
	0.50	c							
yellow, sweet, on the cob	100.00	g	86	3.3	18.7	15.00	270.00	89.00	1.35
	154.00	g	77	2.9	16.8	13.50	243.00	80.10	1.22
	1.00	c							
yello, sweet, creamed, canned	100.00	g	72	1.7	18.1	261.00	134.00	51.00	0.42
	128.00	g	92	2.2	23.2	334.08	171.52	65.28	0.54
	0.50	c							
yellow, sweet, kernels, frozen	100.00	g	88	3.0	20.7	3.00	213.00	70.00	0.78
	82.00	g	72	2.5	17.0	2.46	174.66	57.40	0.64
	0.50	c							
yellow, sweet, canned with liquid	100.00	g	61	2.0	13.9	195.00	136.00	46.00	0.77
	128.00	g	78	2.5	17.7	249.60	174.08	58.88	0.99
	0.50	c							
tortilla, no salt added	100.00	g	222	5.7	46.6	11.00	154.00	314.00	2.50
	26.00	g	58	1.5	12.1	2.86	40.04	81.64	0.65
	1.00	pc							

	SERVING QUANTITY	SERVING UNIT	CALORIES (kcal)	PROTEIN (g)	TOTAL CARBOHYDRATES (g)	SODIUM (mg)	POTASSIUM (mg)	PHOSPHORUS (mg)	TOTAL FAT (g)
BROCCOLI									
florets, raw	100.00	g	28	3.0	5.1	27.00	325.00	66.00	0.35
	71.00	g	20	2.1	3.6	19.17	230.75	46.86	0.25
	1.00	c							
Cooked, no salt	100.00	g	35	2.4	7.2	41.00	293.00	67.00	0.41
	78.00	g	27	1.9	5.6	31.98	228.54	52.26	0.32
	0.50	c							
frozen, spears	100.00	g	29	3.1	5.4	17.00	250.00	59.00	0.34
	85.05	g	25	2.6	4.6	14.46	212.62	50.18	0.29
	3.00	oz							
CAULIFLOWER									
green, raw	100.00	g	31	3.0	6.1	23.00	300.00	62.00	0.30
	64.00	g	20	1.9	3.9	14.72	192.00	39.68	0.19
	1.00	c							
cooked, no salt	100.00	g	32	3.0	6.3	23.00	278.00	57.00	0.31
	62.00	g	20	1.9	3.9	14.26	172.36	35.34	0.19
	0.50	c							
CUCUMBER									
sliced, raw	100.00	g	15	0.7	3.6	2.00	147.00	24.00	0.11
	52.00	g	8	0.3	1.9	1.04	76.44	12.48	0.06
	0.50	c							
sliced	100.00	g	15	0.7	3.6	2.00	147.00	24.00	0.11
	78.00	g	12	0.5	2.8	1.56	114.66	18.72	0.09
	0.75	c							
BEETS									
raw	100.00	g	43	1.6	9.6	78.00	325.00	40.00	0.17
	90.67	g	39	1.5	8.7	70.72	294.67	36.27	0.15
	0.67	c							
whole or sliced, boiled, drained, no salt	100.00	g	44	1.7	10.0	77.00	305.00	38.00	0.18
whole, canned	100.00	g	30	0.7	7.1	143.00	159.00	15.00	0.09
	246.00	g	74	1.8	17.6	351.78	391.14	36.90	0.22
	1.00	c							
sliced, canned, drained	100.00	g	31	0.9	7.2	194.00	148.00	17.00	0.14
	85.00	g	26	0.8	6.1	164.90	125.80	14.45	0.12
	0.50	c							

PEAS

	SERVING QUANTITY	SERVING UNIT	CALORIES (kcal)	PROTEIN (g)	TOTAL CARBOHYDRATES (g)	SODIUM (mg)	POTASSIUM (mg)	PHOSPHORUS (mg)	TOTAL FAT (g)
green	100.00	g	81	5.4	14.5	5.00	244.00	108.00	0.40
	72.50	g	59	3.9	10.5	3.63	176.90	78.30	0.29
	0.50	c							
green, frozen	100.00	g	77	5.2	13.6	108.00	153.00	82.00	0.40
	72.00	g	55	3.8	9.8	77.76	110.16	59.04	0.29
	0.50	c							
green, boiled, drained	100.00	g	84	5.4	15.6	3.00	271.00	117.00	0.22
	80.00	g	67	4.3	12.5	2.40	216.80	93.60	0.18
	0.50	c							
green, canned, drained	100.00	g	68	4.5	11.4	273.00	106.00	67.00	0.80
	87.50	g	60	3.9	9.9	238.88	92.75	58.63	0.70
	0.50	c							
green, frozen, boiled, drained	100.00	g	78	5.2	14.3	72.00	110.00	77.00	0.27
	80.00	g	62	4.1	11.4	57.60	88.00	61.60	0.22
	0.50	c							
split, boiled, no salt added	100.00	g	118	8.3	21.1	2.00	362.00	99.00	0.39
	98.00	g	116	8.2	21.0	1.96	354.76	97.02	0.38
	0.50	c							
sugar or snow peas, whole fresh	100.00	g	42	2.8	7.6	4.00	200.00	53.00	0.20
	78.75	g	33	2.2	6.0	3.15	157.50	41.74	0.16
	1.25	c							
snow/sugar, frozen	100.00	g	42	2.8	7.6	4.00	200.00	53.00	0.20
	78.75	g	33	2.2	6.0	3.15	157.50	41.74	0.16
	1.25	c							
snow/sugar, boiled, drained	100.00	g	42	3.3	7.1	4.00	240.00	55.00	0.23
	80.00	g	34	2.6	5.6	3.20	192.00	44.00	0.18
	0.50	c							
snow/sugar, frozen, boiled, drained	100.00	g	52	3.5	9.0	5.00	217.00	58.00	0.38
	80.00	g	42	2.8	7.2	4.00	173.60	46.40	0.30
	0.50	c							

POTATOES	SERVING QUANTITY	SERVING UNIT	CALORIES (kCal)	PROTEIN (g)	TOTAL CARBOHYDRATES (g)	SODIUM (mg)	POTASSIUM (mg)	PHOSPHORUS (mg)	TOTAL FAT (g)
russet, flesh and skin	100.00	g	79	2.1	18.1	5.00	417.00	55.00	0.08
russet, flesh and skin, baked	100.00	g	95	2.6	21.4	14.00	550.00	71.00	0.13
	173.00	g	164	4.6	37.1	24.22	951.50	122.83	0.22
	1.00	pc							
white, flesh and skin	100.00	g	69	1.7	15.7	16.00	407.00	62.00	0.10
white, flesh and skin, baked	100.00	g	92	2.1	21.1	7.00	544.00	75.00	0.15
	173.00	g	159	3.6	36.5	12.11	941.12	129.75	0.26
	1.00	pcs							
french fries, frozen	100.00	g	147	2.2	24.8	332.00	408.00	83.00	4.66
	71.50	g	105	1.6	17.7	237.38	291.72	59.35	3.33
	11.00	pcs							
sweet, cubed	100.00	g	86	1.6	20.1	55.00	337.00	47.00	0.05
	99.75	g	86	1.6	20.1	54.86	336.16	46.88	0.05
	0.75	c							
sweet, boiled, mashed	100.00	g	76	1.4	17.7	27.00	230.00	32.00	0.14
	328.00	g	249	4.5	58.1	88.56	754.40	104.96	0.46
	1.00	c							
sweet, frozen, baked	100.00	g	100	1.7	23.4	8.00	377.00	44.00	0.12
	117.33	g	117	2.0	27.5	9.39	442.35	51.63	0.14
	0.67	c							
sweet, baked, peeled	100.00	g	90	2.0	20.7	36.00	475.00	54.00	0.15
	0.50	c							
chips, unsalted	100.00	g	536	7.0	52.9	8.00	1,275	165.00	34.60
	28.35	g	152	2.0	15.0	2.27	361.46	46.78	9.81
	1.00	oz							
hash browns, frozen	100.00	g	82	2.1	17.7	22.00	285.00	47.00	0.62
	70.00	g	57	1.4	12.4	15.40	199.50	32.90	0.43
	0.33	c							
wedges, frozen	100.00	g	129	2.7	25.5	49.00	394.00	87.00	2.20

ARTI-CHOKES	SERVING QUANTITY	SERVING UNIT	CALORIES (kcal)	PROTEIN (g)	TOTAL CARBOHYDRATES (g)	SODIUM (mg)	POTASSIUM (mg)	PHOSPHORUS (mg)	TOTAL FAT (g)
whole, boiled, drained med size	100.00	g	53	2.9	12.0	60.00	286	73.00	0.34
	120.00	g	64	3.5	14.3	72.00	343	87.60	0.41
	1.00	pc							
hearts, boiled, drained	100.00	g	53	2.9	11.9	60.00	286	73.00	0.34
	84.00	g	45	2.4	10.0	50.40	240	61.32	0.29
	0.50	c							
Globe or French, frozen boiled, drained	100.00	g	45	3.1	9.2	53.00	264	61.00	0.50
	80.00	g	36	2.5	7.3	42.40	211	48.80	0.40
1 svg= 1/3 of 9oz package	1.00	svg							

ALFALFA

sprouts	100.00	g	23	4.0	2.1	6.00	79.00	70.00	0.69
	33.00	g	8	1.3	0.7	1.98	26.07	23.10	0.23
	1.00	c							

CELERY

stalk medium 7.5 - 8 in long	100.00	g	14	0.7	3.0	80.00	260	24.00	0.17
	80.00	g	11	0.6	2.4	64.00	208	19.20	0.14
	2.00	stalks							
diced, chopped	100.00	g	14	0.7	3.0	80.00	260	24.00	0.17
	101.00	g	14	0.7	3.0	80.80	263	24.24	0.17
	1.00	c							
celeriac or celery root	100.00	g	42	1.5	9.2	100.00	300	115	0.30
	78.00	g	33	1.2	7.2	78.00	234	90	0.23
	0.50	c							
seeds	100.00	g	392	18.1	41.4	160.00	1,400	547	25.27
	2.00	g	8	0.4	0.8	3.20	28.00	10.94	0.51
	1.00	tsp							
flakes, dried	100.00	g	319	11.3	68.7	1,435.00	4,388	402	2.10
	28.35	g	90	3.2	18.1	406.82	1,244	114	0.60
	1.00	oz							

	SERVING QUANTITY	SERVING UNIT	CALORIES (Kcal)	PROTEIN (g)	TOTAL CARBOHYDRATES (g)	SODIUM (mg)	POTASSIUM (mg)	PHOSPHORUS (mg)	TOTAL FAT (g)
COLLARDS									
chopped, raw	100.00	g	32	3.0	5.4	17.00	213.00	25.00	0.61
	90.00	g	29	2.7	4.9	15.30	191.70	22.50	0.55
	2.50	c							
boiled, drained	100.00	g	33	2.7	5.7	15.00	117.00	32.00	0.72
	95.00	g	31	2.6	5.4	14.25	111.15	30.40	0.68
	0.50	c							
frozen, chopped, raw	100.00	g	33	2.7	6.5	48.00	253.00	27.00	0.37
	85.05	g	28	2.3	5.5	40.82	215.17	22.96	0.31
	3.00	oz							
frozen, chopped, boiled/ drained	100.00	g	36	3.0	7.1	50.00	251.00	27.00	0.41
	85.00	g	31	2.5	6.0	42.50	213.35	22.95	0.35
	0.50	c							
EGGPLANT/AUBERGINE									
boiled, drained, no salt	100.00	g	35	0.8	8.7	1.00	123.00	15.00	0.23
	99.00	g	35	0.8	8.6	0.99	121.77	14.85	0.23
cut in 1" cubes	1.00	c							
pickled	100.00	g	49	0.9	9.8	1,674	12.00	9.00	0.70
	136	g	67	1.2	13.3	2,276	16.32	12.24	0.95
	1.00	c							
JICAMA (YAMBEAN)									
raw	100.00	g	38	0.7	8.8	4.00	150.00	18.00	0.09
	86.67	g	33	0.6	7.6	3.47	130.00	15.60	0.08
	0.67	c							
boiled, drained, no salt	100.00	g	38	0.7	8.8	4.00	135.00	16.00	0.09
	85.05	g	32	0.6	7.5	3.40	114.82	13.61	0.08
1 svg= 3oz	3.00	oz							

ARUGULA

	SERVING QUANTITY	SERVING UNIT	CALORIES (kcal)	PROTEIN (g)	TOTAL CARBOHYDRATES (g)	SODIUM (mg)	POTASSIUM (mg)	PHOSPHORUS (mg)	TOTAL FAT (g)
raw, leaves	100	g	25	2.6	3.7	27.00	369	52.00	0.66
	80.00	g	20	2.1	2.9	21.60	295	41.60	0.53
	4.00	c							
salad mixed	100	g	18	1.5	3.3	16.94	299	32.15	0.27
baby greens	41.25	g	7	0.6	1.4	6.99	123	13.26	0.11
Arugula,butterhead, endives, Radicchio	1.00	c							

ENDIVE OR ESCAROLE

raw, chopped	100	g	17	1.3	3.4	22.00	314.00	28.00	0.20
	87.50	g	15	1.1	2.9	19.25	274.75	24.50	0.18
	1.75	c							
Chicory, Witlof	100	g	17	0.9	4.0	2.00	211.00	26.00	0.10
or Belgium	90.00	g	15	0.8	3.6	1.80	189.90	23.40	0.09
	1.00	c							

OKRA

raw	100	g	33	1.9	7.5	7.00	299.00	61.00	0.19
	75.00	g	25	1.5	5.6	5.25	224.25	45.75	0.14
	0.75	c							
sliced, boiled, drained, n.s.	100	g	22	1.9	4.5	6.00	135.00	32.00	0.21
	80.00	g	18	1.5	3.6	4.80	108.00	25.60	0.17
	0.50	c							
frozen	100	g	30	1.7	6.6	3.00	211.00	42.00	0.25
	85.05	g	26	1.4	5.6	2.55	179.45	35.72	0.21
	3.00	oz							
frozen, boiled, drained, no salt sliced	100	g	29	1.6	6.4	3.00	184.00	37.00	0.24
	92.00	g	27	1.5	5.9	2.76	169.28	34.04	0.22
	0.50	c							

PUMPKIN

fruit/meat, raw, cut 1" cube	100	g	26	1.0	6.5	1.00	340.00	44.00	0.10
	116	g	30	1.2	7.5	1.16	394.40	51.04	0.12
	1.00	c							
boiled, drained, mashed, n.s.	100	g	20	0.7	4.9	1.00	230.00	30.00	0.07
	122.5	g	25	0.9	6.0	1.23	281.75	36.75	0.09
	0.50	c							
flowers	100	g	15	0.0	3.3	5.00	173.00	49.00	0.07
	33.00	g	1	0.0	0.1	0.20	6.92	1.96	0.00
	1.00	c							
flowers, boiled, drained	100	g	15	1.1	3.3	6.00	106.00	34.00	0.08
	89.33	g	13	1.0	3.0	5.36	5.36	30.37	0.07
	0.67	c							
seeds (squash kernels), dried	100	g	559	30.2	10.7	7.00	809.00	1,233	49.05
	34.50	g	193	10.4	3.7	2.42	279.11	425.4	16.92
	0.25	c							
seeds (pumkin/squash), whole, roasted no salt added	100	g	446	18.6	53.8	18.00	919.00	92.00	19.40
	32.00	g	143	5.9	17.2	5.76	294.08	29.44	6.21
	0.50	c							

SQUASH

	SERVING QUANTITY	SERVING UNIT	CALORIES (kCal)	PROTEIN (g)	TOTAL CARBOHYDRATES (g)	SODIUM (mg)	POTASSIUM (mg)	PHOSPHORUS (mg)	TOTAL FAT (g)
winter,	100.00	g	34	1.0	8.6	4.00	350.00	23.00	0.13
all varieties cubes	116.00	g	39	1.1	10.0	4.64	406.00	26.68	0.15
	1.00	c							
butternut	100.00	g	45	1.0	11.7	4.00	352.00	33.00	0.10
cubes	140.00	g	63	1.4	16.4	5.60	492.80	46.20	0.14
	1.00	c							
winter,	100.00	g	57	1.8	14.4	2.00	212.00	22.00	0.10
butternut, frozen	85.05	g	48	1.5	12.3	1.70	180.30	18.71	0.09
	3.00	oz							
summer,	100.00	g	16	1.2	3.4	2.00	262.00	38.00	0.18
all varieties sliced	84.75	g	14	1.0	2.8	1.70	222.05	32.21	0.15
	0.75	c							

KOHLRABI

raw	100.00	g	27	1.7	6.2	20.00	350.00	46.00	0.10
	135.00	g	36	2.3	8.4	27.00	472.50	62.10	0.14
	1.00	c							
boiled,	100.00	g	29	1.8	6.7	21.00	340.00	45.00	0.11
drained, sliced	165.00	g	48	3.0	11.0	34.65	561.00	74.25	0.18
	1.00	c							

LEEKS

raw	100.00	g	61	1.5	14.2	20.00	180.00	35.00	0.30
	89.00	g	54	1.3	12.6	17.80	160.20	31.15	0.27
	1.00	c							
boiled, drained,	100.00	g	31	0.8	7.6	10.00	87.00	17.00	0.20
chopped or diced	26.00	g	8	0.2	2.0	2.60	22.62	4.42	0.05
	0.25	c							

CASSAVA/YUCCA/MANIOC

raw	100.00	g	160	1.4	38.1	14.00	271.00	27.00	0.28
	103.00	g	165	1.4	39.2	14.42	279.13	27.81	0.29
	0.50	c							

RADISH

oriental (Daikon), 7" long	100.00	g	18	0.6	4.1	21.00	227.00	23.00	0.10
	338.00	g	61	2.0	13.9	70.98	767.26	77.74	0.34
	1.00	pc							
oriental, boiled, drained, no salt sliced	100.00	g	17	0.7	3.4	13.00	285.00	24.00	0.24
	73.50	g	13	0.5	2.5	9.56	209.48	17.64	0.18
	0.50	c							
sprouts	100.00	g	43	3.8	3.6	6.00	86.00	113.0	2.53
	38.00	g	16	1.5	1.4	2.28	32.68	42.94	0.96
	1.00	c							

SWISS CHARD	SERVING QUANTITY	SERVING UNIT	CALORIES (Kcal)	PROTEIN (g)	TOTAL CARBOHYDRATES (g)	SODIUM (mg)	POTASSIUM (mg)	PHOSPHORUS (mg)	TOTAL FAT (g)
raw	100.00	g	19	1.8	3.7	213.00	379.00	46.00	0.20
	36.00	g	7	0.7	1.4	76.68	136.44	16.56	0.07
	1.00	c							
boiled, drained, no salt	100.00	g	20	1.9	4.1	179.00	549.00	33.00	0.08
	175.00	g	35	3.3	7.2	313.25	960.75	57.75	0.14
	1.00	c							
SPINACH									
raw, chopped	100.00	g	23	2.9	3.6	79.00	558.00	49.00	0.39
	90.00	g	21	2.6	3.3	71.10	502.20	44.10	0.35
	3.00	c							
frozen	100.00	g	29	3.6	4.2	74.00	346.00	49.00	0.57
	78.00	g	23	2.8	3.3	57.72	269.88	38.22	0.44
	0.50	c							
chopped, boiled, drained, no salt	100.00	g	23	3.0	3.8	70.00	466.00	56.00	0.26
	90.00	g	21	2.7	3.4	63.00	419.40	50.40	0.23
	0.50	c							
mustard (Tendergreens)	100.00	g	22	2.2	3.9	21.00	449.00	28.00	0.30
	150.00	g	33	3.3	5.9	31.50	673.50	42.00	0.45
	1.00	c							
mustard, boiled, drained, no salt	100.00	g	16	1.7	2.8	14.00	285.00	18.00	0.20
	180.00	g	29	3.1	5.0	25.20	513.00	32.40	0.36
	1.00	c							
TOMATILLOS									
chopped	100.00	g	32	1.0	5.8	1.00	268.00	39.00	1.02
	132.00	g	42	1.3	7.7	1.32	353.76	51.48	1.35
	1.00	c							
TURNIPS									
raw	100.00	g	28	0.9	6.4	67.00	191.00	27.00	0.10
	130.00	g	34	1.1	7.8	81.74	233.02	32.94	0.12
	1.00	c							
frozen	100.00	g	16	1.0	2.9	25.00	137.00	20.00	0.16
	85.05	g	14	0.9	2.5	21.26	116.52	17.01	0.14
	3.00	oz							
cubed, boiled, drained, no salt	100.00	g	22	0.7	5.1	16.00	177.00	40.56	0.08
	156.00	g	34	1.1	7.9	24.96	276.12	26.00	0.12
	1.00	c							
frozen, boiled, drained, no salt	100.00	g	23	1.5	4.4	36.00	182.00	26.00	0.24
	78.00	g	18	1.2	3.4	28.08	141.96	20.28	0.19
	0.50	c							

	SERVING QUANTITY	SERVING UNIT	CALORIES (kCal)	PROTEIN (g)	TOTAL CARBOHYDRATES (g)	SODIUM (mg)	POTASSIUM (mg)	PHOSPHORUS (mg)	TOTAL FAT (g)
TURNIP GREENS									
raw, turnip greens, chopped	100.00	g	32	1.5	7.1	40.00	296.00	42.00	0.30
	82.50	g	26	1.2	5.9	33.00	244.20	34.65	0.25
	1.50	c							
frozen	100.00	g	22	2.5	3.7	12.00	184.00	27.00	0.31
	82.00	g	18	2.0	3.0	9.84	150.88	22.14	0.25
	0.50	c							
canned	100.00	g	14	1.4	2.4	277.00	141.00	21.00	0.30
	78.00	g	11	1.1	1.9	216.06	109.98	16.38	0.23
	0.33	c							
chopped, boiled, drained, no salt	100.00	g	20	1.1	4.4	29.00	203.00	29.00	0.23
	144.00	g	29	1.6	6.3	41.76	292.32	41.76	0.33
	1.00	c							
canned, with no salt	100.00	g	19	1.4	2.8	29.00	141.00	21.00	0.30
	144.00	g	27	2.0	4.1	41.76	203.04	30.24	0.43
	1.00	c							
frozen, chopped, boiled, drained, no salt added	100.00	g	29	3.4	5.0	15.00	224.00	34.00	0.42
	164.00	g	48	5.5	8.2	24.60	367.36	55.76	0.69
	1.00	c							
RUTABAGA									
raw, cubes	100.00	g	37	1.1	8.6	12.00	305.00	53.00	0.16
	93.33	g	35	1.0	8.1	11.20	284.67	49.47	0.15
	0.67	c							
boiled, drained, no salt cubed	100.00	g	30	0.9	6.8	5.00	216.00	41.00	0.18
	170.00	g	51	1.6	11.6	8.50	367.20	69.70	0.31
	1.00	c							
boiled, drained, mashed	100.00	g	30	0.9	6.8	5.00	216.00	41.00	0.18
	160.80	g	48	1.5	11.0	8.04	347.33	65.93	0.29
	0.67	c							
PARSNIPS									
raw, sliced	100.00	g	75	1.2	18.0	10.00	375.00	71.00	0.30
	88.67	g	67	1.1	16.0	8.87	332.50	62.95	0.27
	0.67	c							
boiled, drained, sliced, no salt	100.00	g	71	1.3	17.0	10.00	367.00	69.00	0.30
	78.00	g	55	1.0	13.3	7.80	286.26	53.82	0.23
	0.50	c							

WATER CHESTNUTS	SERVING QUANTITY	SERVING UNIT	CALORIES (Kcal)	PROTEIN (g)	TOTAL CARBOHYDRATES (g)	SODIUM (mg)	POTASSIUM (mg)	PHOSPHORUS (mg)	TOTAL FAT (g)
fresh, raw,	100.00	g	97	1.4	23.9	14.00	584.00	63.00	0.10
Chinese (Matai) slices	62.00	g	60	0.9	14.8	8.68	362.08	39.06	0.06
	0.50	c							
canned with	100.00	g	50	0.9	12.3	8.00	118.00	19.00	0.06
liquid Chinese (Matai)	70.00	g	35	0.6	8.6	5.60	82.60	13.30	0.04
	0.50	c							
WATERCRESS									
raw, chopped	100.00	g	11	2.3	1.3	41.00	330.00	60.00	0.10
	34.00	g	4	0.8	0.4	13.94	112.20	20.40	0.03
	1.00	c							
YAM									
raw, in cubes	100.00	g	118	1.5	28.0	9.00	816.00	55.00	0.17
	112.50	g	133	1.7	31.4	10.13	918.00	61.88	0.19
	0.75	c							
baked or	100.00	g	116	1.5	27.5	8.00	670.00	49.00	0.14
broiled, drained, no salt cubed	68.00	g	79	1.0	18.7	5.44	455.60	33.32	0.10
	0.50	c							
Hawaiin	100.00	g	67	1.3	16.3	13.00	418.00	34.00	0.10
Mountain, raw cubed	68.00	g	46	0.9	11.1	8.84	284.24	23.12	0.07
	0.50	c							
Hawaiian	100.00	g	82	1.7	20.0	12.00	495.00	40.00	0.08
Mountain, steamed cubed	145.00	g	119	2.5	29.0	17.40	717.75	58.00	0.12
	1.00	c							
MIXED VEGETABLES									
frozen	100.00	g	72	3.3	13.5	47.00	212.00	59.00	0.52
	72.00	g	52	2.4	9.7	33.84	152.64	42.48	0.37
	0.50	c							
frozen, boiled,	100.00	g	65	2.9	13.1	35.00	169.00	51.00	0.15
drained, no salt added	91.00	g	59	2.6	11.9	31.85	153.79	46.41	0.14
	0.50	c							
canned,	100.00	g	49	2.6	9.3	214.00	291.00	42.00	0.25
drained	163.00	g	80	4.2	15.1	348.82	474.33	68.46	0.41
	1.00	c							
BRUSSEL SPROUTS									
raw	100.00	g	43	33.4	9.0	25.00	389.00	69.00	0.30
	88.00	g	38	3.0	7.9	22.00	342.00	60.70	0.26
	1.00	c							

	SERVING QUANTITY	SERVING UNIT	CALORIES (kCal)	PROTEIN (g)	TOTAL CARBOHYDRATES (g)	SODIUM (mg)	POTASSIUM (mg)	PHOSPHORUS (mg)	TOTAL FAT (g)
KALE									
raw, chopped	100.00	g	35	2.9	4.4	53.00	348.00	55.00	1.49
	83.75	g	29	2.5	3.7	44.39	291.45	46.06	1.25
	1.25	c							
chopped,	100.00	g	36	2.9	5.3	16.00	144.00	42.00	1.21
boiled, drained, no salt	65.00	g	23	1.9	3.5	10.40	93.60	27.30	0.79
	0.50	c							
scotch, raw, chopped	100.00	g	42	2.8	8.3	70.00	450.00	62.00	0.60
	83.75	g	35	2.4	7.0	58.63	376.88	51.93	0.50
	1.25	c							
scotch, boiled, drained, chopped no salt	100.00	g	28	1.9	5.6	45.00	274.00	38.00	0.41
	86.67	g	24	1.7	4.9	39.00	237.47	32.93	0.36
	0.67	c							
frozen, raw 1 pack=10 oz/ 284g	100.00	g	28	2.7	4.9	15.00	333.00	29.00	0.46
	85.05	g	24	2.3	4.2	12.76	283.21	24.66	0.39
	3.00	oz							
frozen, chopped, boiled, drained, no salt	100.00	g	36	2.9	5.3	16.00	144.00	42.00	1.21
	65.00	g	23	1.9	3.5	10.40	93.60	27.30	0.79
	0.50	c							
MUSTARD GREENS									
raw, chopped	100.00	g	27	2.9	4.7	20.00	384.00	58.00	0.42
	84.00	g	23	2.4	3.9	16.80	322.56	48.72	0.35
	1.50	c							
boiled, drained, chopped, no salt	100.00	g	26	2.6	4.5	9.00	162.00	42.00	0.47
	70.00	g	18	1.8	3.2	6.30	113.40	29.40	0.33
	0.50	c							
frozen 1 pack=10oz/284g	100.00	g	20	2.5	3.4	29.00	170.00	30.00	0.27
	73.00	g	15	1.8	2.5	21.17	124.10	21.90	0.20
	0.50	c							
frozen, boiled, drained, no salt 1 pack = 10oz/ 212g	100.00	g	19	2.3	3.1	25.00	139.00	24.00	0.25
	75.00	g	14	1.7	2.3	18.75	104.25	18.00	0.19
	0.50	c							

B. Vegetable Proteins

Hey there!

Do you need to print out this Food List?

You can download a printable version of this chart by scanning the QR code below or copying the link on your computer browser.

https://go.renaltracker.com/printfoodlist

BEANS

	SERVING QUANTITY	SERVING UNIT	CALORIES (kCal)	PROTEIN (g)	TOTAL CARBOHYDRATES (g)	SODIUM (mg)	POTASSIUM (mg)	PHOSPHORUS (mg)	TOTAL FAT (g)
Lentils/Pinto/	100.00	g	131	8.6	23.9	1.67	398.91	165.76	0.49
Navy	92.00	g	121	8.0	22.0	1.54	367.00	152.50	0.45
	0.50	c							
Lima	100.00	g	113	6.8	20.2	8.00	467.00	136.00	0.86
	78.00	g	88	5.3	15.7	6.24	364.26	106.08	0.67
	0.50	c							
Broad or	100.00	g	72	5.6	11.7	50.00	250.00	95.00	0.60
Fava	81.75	g	59	4.6	9.6	40.88	204.38	77.66	0.49
	0.75	c							
Black beans,	100.00	g	132	8.9	23.7	1.00	355.00	140.00	0.54
boiled	86.00	g	114	7.6	20.4	0.86	305.30	120.40	0.46
	0.50	c							
Mungo,	100.00	g	105	7.5	18.3	7.00	231.00	156.00	0.55
boiled	90.00	g	95	6.8	16.5	6.30	207.90	140.40	0.50
	0.50	c							
sprouts,	100.00	g	30	3.0	5.9	6.00	149.00	54.00	0.18
Mung	78.00	g	23	2.4	4.6	4.68	116.22	42.12	0.14
	0.75	c							
Kidney,	100.00	g	127	8.7	22.8	1.00	405.00	138.00	0.50
boiled	88.50	g	112	7.7	20.2	0.89	358.43	122.13	0.44
	0.50	c							
Navy, boiled	100.00	g	140	8.2	26.1	0.00	389.00	144.00	0.62
	91.00	g	127	7.5	23.7	0.00	353.99	131.04	0.56
	0.50	c							
Lupin, boiled	100.00	g	119	15.6	9.9	4.00	245.00	128.00	2.92
	83.00	g	99	12.9	8.2	3.32	203.35	106.24	2.42
	0.50	c							
Pinto, frozen	100.00	g	170	9.8	32.5	92.00	755.98	117.00	0.50
	94.49	g	161	9.3	31.0	86.93	714.34	110.55	0.47
	3.33	oz							
Pinto, boiled	100.00	g	143	9.0	26.2	1.00	436.00	147.00	0.65
	85.50	g	122	7.7	22.4	0.86	372.78	125.69	0.56
	0.50	c							
White (Cannellini), boiled no salt	100.00	g	139	9.7	25.1	6.00	561.00	113.00	0.35
	89.50	g	124	8.7	22.5	5.37	502.10	101.14	0.31
	0.50	c							

BEANS	SERVING QUANTITY	SERVING UNIT	CALORIES (kCal)	PROTEIN (g)	TOTAL CARBOHYDRATES (g)	SODIUM (mg)	POTASSIUM (mg)	PHOSPHORUS (mg)	TOTAL FAT (g)
White, small, boiled, no salt	100.00	g	142	9.0	25.8	2.00	463.00	169.00	0.64
	89.50	g	127	8.0	23.1	1.79	414.39	151.26	0.57
	0.50	c							
sprouts, Kidney	100.00	g	29	4.2	4.1	6.00	187.00	37.00	0.50
	92.00	g	27	3.9	3.8	5.52	172.04	34.04	0.46
	0.50	c							
sprouts, Navy	100.00	g	67	6.2	13.1	13.00	307.00	100.00	0.70
	78.00	g	52	4.8	10.2	10.14	239.46	78.00	0.55
	0.75	c							
sprouts, Pinto	100.00	g	62	5.3	11.6	153.0	307.00	94.00	0.90
	85.05	g	53	4.5	9.9	130.1	262.10	79.95	0.77
	3.00	oz							
French, boiled	100.00	g	129	7.1	24.0	6.00	370.00	102.00	0.76
	88.50	g	114	6.2	21.3	5.31	327.45	90.27	0.67
	0.50	c							
baked, prepared	100.00	g	155	5.5	21.6	422.0	358.00	109.00	5.15
	126.50	g	196	7.0	27.4	533.8	452.87	138.00	6.51
	0.50	c							
Refried, canned	100.00	g	90	5.0	13.6	370.0	319.00	92.00	2.01
	119.00	g	107	5.9	16.1	440.3	379.61	109.48	2.39
	0.50	c							

CHICKPEAS

	SERVING QUANTITY	SERVING UNIT	CALORIES (kCal)	PROTEIN (g)	TOTAL CARBOHYDRATES (g)	SODIUM (mg)	POTASSIUM (mg)	PHOSPHORUS (mg)	TOTAL FAT (g)
garbanzos/ bengal gram, canned	100.00	g	88	4.9	13.5	278.0	144.00	80.00	1.95
	120.00	g	106	5.9	16.2	333.6	172.80	96.00	2.34
	0.50	c							
garbanzos/ bengal gram, boiled	100.00	g	164	8.9	27.4	7.00	291.00	168.00	2.59
	82.00	g	134	7.3	22.5	5.74	238.62	137.76	2.12
	0.50	c							
garbanzos/ bengal gram, canned drained, rinsed in tap water	100.00	g	138	7.0	22.9	212.0	109.00	80.00	2.47
	152.00	g	210	10.7	34.8	322.3	165.68	121.60 ·	3.75
	1.00	c							
garbanzos/ bengal gram, canned low sodium	100	g	88	4.9	13.5	132.0	144.00	80.00	1.95
	240	g	211	11.8	32.4	316.8	345.60	192.00	4.68
	1	c							
flour	100.00	g	387	22.4	57.8	64.00	846.00	318.00	6.69
	92.00	g	110	6.4	16.4	18.14	239.84	90.15	1.90
	1.00	c							

Vegetable Proteins

	SERVING QUANTITY	SERVING UNIT	CALORIES (kCal)	PROTEIN (g)	TOTAL CARBOHYDRATES (g)	SODIUM (mg)	POTASSIUM (mg)	PHOSPHORUS (mg)	TOTAL FAT (g)
TOFU									
soft with calcium sulfate and magnesium chloride (Nigari)	100.00	g	61	7.2	1.2	8.00	120.00	92.00	3.69
	85.05	g	52	6.1	1.0	6.80	102.06	78.25	3.14
	3.00	oz							
firm with calcium sulfate and magnesium chloride (Nigari)	100.00	g	78	9.0	2.9	12.00	148.00	121.00	4.17
	85.05	g	66	7.7	2.4	10.21	125.87	102.91	3.55
	3.00	oz							
silken tofu (Vitasoy USA)	100.00	g	43	4.8	0.6	2.00	na	na	2.40
	91.00	g	39	4.4	0.5	1.82	na	na	2.18
	0.20	package							
TEMPEH									
raw	100.00	g	192	20.3	7.6	9.00	412.0	266.0	10.80
	83.00	g	159	16.8	6.3	7.47	341.9	220.8	8.96
	0.50	c							
cooked	100.00	g	185	19.9	7.6	14.00	401.0	253.0	11.38
EDAMAME									
frozen, unprepared	100.00	g	109	11.2	7.6	6.00	482.0	161.0	4.73
	118.00	g	129	13.2	9.0	7.08	568.7	189.9	5.58
	1.00	c							
frozen, prepared	100.00	g	121	11.9	8.9	6.00	436.0	261.9	5.20
	155.00	g	188	18.5	13.8	9.30	676	169	8.06
	1.00	c							
SPIRULINA									
seaweed, fresh/raw	100.00	g	26	5.9	2.4	98.00	127	11.00	0.39
	28.35	g	7	1.7	0.7	27.78	36.00	3.12	0.11
	1.00	oz							
seaweed, dried	100.00	g	290	57.5	23.9	1,048	1363	118	7.72
	112.00	g	325	64.4	26.8	1,174	1527	133	8.65
	1.00	c							

C. Fruits

Hey there!

Do you need to print out this Food List?

You can download a printable version of this chart by scanning the QR code below or copying the link on your computer browser.

https://go.renaltracker.com/printfoodlist

APPLE

	SERVING QUANTITY	SERVING UNIT	CALORIES (kCal)	PROTEIN (g)	TOTAL CARBOHYDRATES (g)	SODIUM (mg)	POTASSIUM (mg)	PHOSPHORUS (mg)	TOTAL FAT (g)
Gala, raw, with skin	100.00	g	57	0.3	13.7	1.00	108.00	11.00	0.12
	172.00	g	98	0.4	23.5	1.72	185.76	18.92	0.21
	1.00	pc, med							
fuji, raw, with skin	100.00	g	63	0.2	15.2	1.00	109.00	13.00	0.18
	192.00	g	121	0.4	29.2	1.92	209.28	24.96	0.35
	1.00	pc, med							
golden delicious, with skin	100.00	g	57	0.3	13.6	2.00	100.00	10.00	0.15
	169.00	g	96	0.5	23.0	3.38	169.00	16.90	0.25
	1.00	pc, med							
granny smith, w/ skin, raw	100.00	g	58	0.4	13.6	1.00	120.00	12.00	0.19
	167.00	g	97	0.7	22.7	1.67	200.40	20.04	0.32
	1.00	pc, med							
juice, frozen concentrate	100.00	g	47	0.1	11.5	7.00	126.00	7.00	0.10
	239.00	g	112	0.3	27.6	16.73	301.14	16.73	0.24
	8.00	fl oz							
applesauce, sweetened, canned	100.00	g	68	0.2	17.5	2.00	75.00	6.00	0.17
	123.00	g	84	0.2	21.5	2.46	92.25	7.38	0.21
	0.50	c							
applesauce, unsweetened, canned	100.00	g	42	0.2	11.3	2.00	74.00	5.00	0.10
	122.00	g	51	0.2	13.8	2.44	90.28	6.10	0.12
	0.50	c							

BLACK BERRIES

	SERVING QUANTITY	SERVING UNIT	CALORIES (kCal)	PROTEIN (g)	TOTAL CARBOHYDRATES (g)	SODIUM (mg)	POTASSIUM (mg)	PHOSPHORUS (mg)	TOTAL FAT (g)
raw	100.00	g	43	1.4	9.6	1.00	162.00	22.00	0.49
	144.00	g	62	2.0	13.8	1.44	233.28	31.68	0.71
	1.00	c							
frozen, unsweetened	100.00	g	64	1.2	15.7	1.00	140.00	30.00	0.43
	151.00	g	97	1.8	23.7	1.51	211.40	45.30	0.65
	1.00	c							
canned, heavy syrup	100.00	g	92	1.3	23.1	3.00	99.00	14.00	0.14
	256.00	g	236	3.4	59.1	7.68	253.44	35.84	0.36
	1.00	c							

RASP BERRIES	SERVING QUANTITY	SERVING UNIT	CALORIES (KCal)	PROTEIN (g)	TOTAL CARBOHYDRATES (g)	SODIUM (mg)	POTASSIUM (mg)	PHOSPHORUS (mg)	TOTAL FAT (g)
raw	100.00	g	52	1.2	11.9	1.00	151.00	29.00	0.69
	123.00	g	64	1.5	14.7	1.23	185.73	35.67	0.80
	1.00	c							
frozen, unsweetend	100.00	g	56	1.2	12.6	4.00	184.00	30.00	0.81
	140.00	g	78	1.6	17.6	5.60	257.60	42.00	1.13
	1.00	c							
red, frozen, sweetened, unthawed	100.00	g	103	0.7	26.2	1.00	114.00	17.00	0.16
	125.00	g	129	0.9	32.7	1.25	142.50	21.25	0.20
	0.50	c							
puree, with seeds	100.00	g	55	na	11.5	4.00	195.00	30.00	0.97
juice concentrate	100.00	g	221	3.0	53.2	10.0	1,178.0	100.0	1.34
PEARS									
whole, medium (2.5/lb)	100.00	g	57	0.4	15.2	1.00	116.00	16.00	0.14
	166.00	g	95	0.6	25.3	1.66	192.56	19.92	0.23
	1.00	pc							
halves, canned in water	100.00	g	29	0.2	7.8	2.00	53.00	7.00	0.03
	244.00	g	71	0.5	19.1	4.88	129.32	17.08	0.07
	1.00	c							
Asian	100.00	g	42	0.5	10.7	0.00	121.00	11.00	0.23
	122.00	g	51	0.6	13.0	0.00	147.62	13.42	0.28
	1.00	pc							
CRANBERRY									
fresh, chopped	100.00	g	46	0.5	12.0	2.00	80.00	11.00	0.13
	55.00	g	25	0.3	6.6	1.10	44.00	6.05	0.07
	0.50	c							
dried, sweetened	100.00	g	308	0.2	82.8	5.00	49.00	8.00	1.09
	40.00	g	123	0.1	33.1	2.00	19.60	3.20	0.44
	0.33	c							
juice, unsweetened	100.00	g	46	0.4	12.2	2.00	77.00	13.00	0.13
	253.00	g	116	1.0	30.9	5.06	194.81	32.89	0.33
	1.00	c							
juice, cran cocktail	100.00	g	54	0.0	13.5	2.00	14.00	1.00	0.10
	253.00	g	137	0.0	34.2	5.06	35.42	2.53	0.25
	8.00	fl oz							
sauce, canned, sweetened	100.00	g	159	0.9	40.4	5.00	28.00	4.00	0.15
	69.25	g	110	0.6	28.0	3.46	19.39	2.77	0.10
	0.25	c							

GRAPE

	SERVING QUANTITY	SERVING UNIT	CALORIES (kCal)	PROTEIN (g)	TOTAL CARBOHYDRATES (g)	SODIUM (mg)	POTASSIUM (mg)	PHOSPHORUS (mg)	TOTAL FAT (g)
red or green, seedless	100.00	g	69	0.7	18.1	2.00	191.00	20.00	0.16
	151.00	g	104	1.1	27.3	3.02	288.41	30.20	0.24
	1.00	c							
juice, unsweetened, plus Vit.C	100.00	g	60	0.4	14.8	5.00	104.00	14.00	0.13
	252.80	g	152	0.9	37.3	12.64	262.90	35.39	0.33
	8.00	fl oz							
fruit mixed/ fruit cocktail, light, drained	100.00	g	55	0.4	14.3	6.00	85.00	13.00	0.08
juice, sweetened, frozen concentrate 6 fl oz can	100.00	g	179	0.7	44.4	7.00	74.00	15.00	0.31
	216.00	g	387	1.4	95.8	15.12	159.84	32.40	0.67
	1.00	can/ item							
seedless, Thompson, canned in water	100.00	g	40	0.5	10.3	6.00	107.00	18.00	0.11
	245.00	g	98	1.2	25.2	14.70	262.15	44.10	0.27
	1.00	c							
jelly 1 packet= 14g (0.5oz)	100.00	g	266	0.2	70.0	30.00	54.00	6.00	0.02
	21.00	g	56	0.0	14.7	6.30	11.34	1.26	0.00
	1	tbsp							

PINE APPLE

	SERVING QUANTITY	SERVING UNIT	CALORIES (kcal)	PROTEIN (g)	TOTAL CARBOHYDRATES (g)	SODIUM (mg)	POTASSIUM (mg)	PHOSPHORUS (mg)	TOTAL FAT (g)
traditional varieties, diced	100.00	g	45	0.6	18.3	1.00	125.00	9.00	0.13
	155.00	g	70	0.9	11.8	1.55	193.75	13.95	0.20
	1.00	c							
sweetened, frozen, chunks	100.00	g	86	0.4	22.2	2.00	100.00	4.00	0.10
	245.00	g	211	1.0	54.4	4.90	245.00	9.80	0.25
	1.00	c							
canned in water crushed, sliced, or chunks	100.00	g	32	0.4	8.3	1.00	127.00	4.00	0.09
	246.00	g	79	1.1	20.4	2.46	312.42	9.84	0.22
	1.00	c							
canned in juice crushed, sliced, or chunks	100.00	g	60	0.4	15.7	1.00	122.00	6.00	0.08
	249.00	g	149	1.1	39.1	2.49	303.78	14.94	0.20
	1.00	c							
extra sweet variety, diced	100.00	g	51	0.5	13.5	1.00	108.00	8.00	0.11
	155.00	g	79	0.8	20.9	1.55	167.40	12.40	0.17
	1.00	c							
juice, unsweetened, canned	100.00	g	53	0.4	12.9	2.00	130.00	8.00	0.12
	250.00	g	133	0.9	32.2	5.00	325.00	20.00	0.30
	8.00	fl oz							
canned in light syrup crushed, sliced, or chunks	100.00	g	52	0.4	13.5	1.00	105.00	7.00	0.12
	126.00	g	66	0.5	17.0	1.26	132.30	8.82	0.15
	0.50	c							
juice, unsweetened, frozen concentrate	100.00	g	179	1.3	44.3	3.00	472.00	28.00	0.10
	288.00	g	387	2.8	95.7	6.48	1,019.5	60.48	0.22
	1.00	c							
juice, 40pprox.40ne d with Vit A, C & E	100.00	g	50	0.4	12.2	3.00	132.00	9.00	0.14
	250.00	g	125	0.9	30.5	7.50	330.00	22.50	0.35
	1.00	c							

BLUE BERRIES

	SERVING QUANTITY	SERVING UNIT	CALORIES (kCal)	PROTEIN (g)	TOTAL CARBOHYDRATES (g)	SODIUM (mg)	POTASSIUM (mg)	PHOSPHORUS (mg)	TOTAL FAT (g)
fresh	100.00	g	57	0.7	14.5	1.00	77.00	12.00	0.33
	145.00	g	83	1.1	21.0	1.45	111.6	17.40	0.48
	1.00	c							
sweetened, dried	100.00	g	317	2.5	80.0	3.00	214.0	36.00	2.50
	40.00	g	127	1.0	32.0	1.20	85.60	14.40	1.00
	0.25	c							
wild, frozen	100.00	g	57	0.0	13.9	3.00	68.00	13.00	0.16
	140.00	g	80	0.0	19.4	4.20	95.20	18.20	0.22
	1.00	c							
unsweetened, frozen	100.00	g	51	0.4	12.2	1.00	54.00	11.00	0.64
	155.00	g	79	0.7	18.9	1.55	83.70	17.05	0.99
	1.00	c							
canned, light syrup , drained	100.00	g	88	1.0	22.7	3.00	54.00	12.00	0.40
	244.00	g	215	2.5	55.3	7.32	131.7	29.28	0.98
	1.00	c							

STRAWBERRIES

	SERVING QUANTITY	SERVING UNIT	CALORIES (kCal)	PROTEIN (g)	TOTAL CARBOHYDRATES (g)	SODIUM (mg)	POTASSIUM (mg)	PHOSPHORUS (mg)	TOTAL FAT (g)
fresh, whole	100.00	g	32	0.7	7.7	1.00	153.0	24.00	0.30
	144.00	g	46	1.0	11.1	1.44	220.3	34.56	0.43
	1.00	c							
unsweetened, frozen (unthawed)	100.00	g	35	0.4	9.1	2.00	148.0	13.00	0.11
	149.00	g	52	0.6	13.6	2.98	220.5	19.37	
									0.16
	1.00	c							
sweetened, frozen, thawed	100.00	g	78	0.5	21.0	1.00	98.00	12.00	0.14
	127.50	g	99	0.7	26.8	1.28	124.9	15.30	0.18
	0.50	c							
fruit topping	100.00	g	254	0.2	66.3	21.00	51.00	5.00	0.10
	42.00	g	107	0.1	27.9	8.82	21.42	2.10	0.04
	2.00	tbsp							
pastry, 41pprox, enriched	100.00	g	371	5.4	47.8	445.00	83.00	89.00	18.50
	71.00	g	263	3.8	33.9	315.95	58.93	63.19	13.14
	1.00	pc							
Milkshake (fastfood)	100.00	g	113	3.4	18.9	83.00	182.0	100.0	2.80
	226.40	g	256	7.7	42.8	187.91	412.1	226.4	6.34
	8.00	fl oz							
yogurt 41ppro, low fat 1 item = 1 container	100.00	g	105	8.2	12.3	33.00	129.0	109.0	2.57
	150.00	g	158	12.3	18.4	49.50	193.5	163.5	3.86
	1.00	item							

GRAPE-FRUIT	SERVING QUANTITY	SERVING UNIT	CALORIES (kcal)	PROTEIN (g)	TOTAL CARBOHYDRATES (g)	SODIUM (mg)	POTASSIUM (mg)	PHOSPHORUS (mg)	TOTAL FAT (g)
fresh	100.00	g	32	0.6	8.1	0.00	139.0	8.00	0.10
	153.33	g	49	1.0	12.4	0.00	213.1	12.27	0.15
	0.67	c							
white, fresh, small (3.5 diameter)	100.00	g	33	0.7	8.4	0.00	148.0	8.00	0.10
	118.00	g	39	0.8	9.9	0.00	174.6	9.44	0.12
	0.50	pc							
pink or red	100.00	g	42	0.8	10.7	0.00	135.0	18.00	0.14
	153.33	g	64	1.2	16.4	0.00	207.0	27.60	0.21
	0.67	c							
juice, white	100.00	g	39	0.5	9.2	1.00	162.0	15.00	0.10
	247.00	g	96	1.2	22.7	2.47	400.2	37.05	0.25
	8.00	fl oz							
juice, pink	100.00	g	39	0.5	9.2	1.00	162.0	15.00	0.10
	247.00	g	96	1.2	22.7	2.47	400.2	37.05	0.25
	1.00	c							
juice, unsweetened, pink, canned	100.00	g	37	0.6	7.5	2.00	141.0	17.00	0.66
	247.20	g	91	1.4	18.6	4.94	348.6	42.02	1.63
	8.00	fl oz							

ELDERBERRIES

	SERVING QUANTITY	SERVING UNIT	CALORIES	PROTEIN	TOTAL CARBOHYDRATES	SODIUM	POTASSIUM	PHOSPHORUS	TOTAL FAT
	100.00	g	73	7.0	18.4	6.00	280.0	39.00	0.50
fresh	145.00	g	106	1.0	26.7	8.70	406.0	56.55	0.73
	1.00	c							

GOOSEBERRIES

fresh	100.00	g	44	0.9	10.2	1.00	198.0	27.00	0.58
	150.00	g	66	1.3	15.3	1.50	297.0	40.50	0.87
	1.00	c							
canned in light syrup	100.00	g	73	0.7	18.8	2.00	77.00	7.00	0.20
	252.00	g	184	1.6	47.3	5.04	194.1	17.64	0.50
	1.00	c							

KIWI (Chinese gooseberries)

fresh, medium, without skin	100.00	g	61	1.1	14.7	3.00	312.0	34.00	0.52
	76.00	g	46	0.9	11.1	2.28	237.1	25.84	0.40
	1.00	pc							

LOGAN BERRIES

frozen	100.00	g	55	1.5	13.0	1.00	145.0	26.00	0.31
	147.00	g	81	2.2	19.1	1.47	213.2	38.22	0.46
	1.00	c							

CHERRIES

	SERVING QUANTITY	SERVING UNIT	CALORIES (KCal)	PROTEIN (g)	TOTAL CARBOHYDRATES (g)	SODIUM (mg)	POTASSIUM (mg)	PHOSPHORUS (mg)	TOTAL FAT (g)
sweet, without pits	100.00	g	63	1.1	16.0	0.00	222.0	21.00	0.20
	154.00	g	97	1.6	24.7	0.00	341.9	32.34	0.31
	1.00	c							
sour red, without pits	100.00	g	50	1.0	12.2	3.00	173.0	15.00	0.30
	155.00	g	78	1.6	18.9	4.65	268.2	23.25	0.47
	1.00	c							
juice, tart	100.00	g	59	0.3	13.7	4.00	161.0	17.00	0.54
	269.00	g	159	0.8	36.9	10.76	433.1	45.73	1.45
	1.00	c							
Pitanga or Surinam	100.00	g	33	0.8	7.5	3.00	103.0	11.00	0.40
	173.00	g	57	1.4	13.0	5.19	178.2	19.03	0.69
	1.00	c							
tart, dried, sweetened	100.00	g	333	1.3	80.5	13.00	376.0	36.00	0.73
	40.00	g	133	0.5	32.2	5.20	150.4	14.40	0.29
	0.25	c							
maraschino, canned, drained	100.00	g	165	0.2	42.0	4.00	21.0	3.00	0.21
	5.00	g	8	0.0	2.1	0.20	1.05	0.15	0.01
	1.00	pc/ item							
sweet, canned in juice, pitted	100.00	g	54	0.9	13.8	3.00	131.0	22.00	0.02
	250.00	g	135	2.3	34.5	7.50	327.5	55.00	0.05
	1.00	c							
sweet, canned in water	100.00	g	46	0.8	11.8	1.00	131.0	15.00	0.13
	248.00	g	114	1.9	29.2	2.48	324.9	37.20	0.32
	1.00	c							
sweet, frozen, sweetened thawed	100.00	g	89	1.2	22.4	1.00	199.0	16.00	0.13
	259.00	g	231	3.0	57.9	2.59	515.4	41.44	0.34
	1.00	c							
pie filling, canned 1/8 of 21 oz can	100.00	g	115	0.4	28.0	18.00	105.0	15.00	0.07
	74.00	g	85	0.3	20.7	13.32	77.70	11.10	0.05
	1.00	svg							
pie fillings, low calorie	100.00	g	53	0.8	12.0	12.00	118.0	15.00	0.16
	264.00	g	140	2.2	31.6	31.68	311.5	39.60	0.42
	1.00	c							
sour red, canned in water, drained	100.00	g	42	0.7	10.5	4.00	115.0	16.00	0.21
	168.00	g	71	1.2	17.6	6.72	193.2	26.88	0.35
	1.00	c							
sour red, 43pprox.43ned, frozen unthawed	100.00	g	46	0.9	11.0	1.00	124.0	16.00	0.44
	155.00	g	71	1.4	17.1	1.55	192.2	24.80	0.68
	1.00	c							
sour red, canned in light syrup	100.00	g	75	0.7	19.3	7.00	95.00	10.00	0.10
	126.00	g	95	0.9	24.3	8.82	119.7	12.60	0.13
	0.50	c							

43

PEACHES

	SERVING QUANTITY	SERVING UNIT	CALORIES (kcal)	PROTEIN (g)	TOTAL CARBOHYDRATES (g)	SODIUM (mg)	POTASSIUM (mg)	PHOSPHORUS (mg)	TOTAL FAT (g)
raw, medium	100.00	g	39	0.9	9.5	0.00	190.0	20.00	0.25
(44pprox. 4/lb)	150.00	g	59	1.4	14.3	0.00	285.0	30.00	0.38
	1.00	pc/ item							
dried	100.00	g	325	4.9	83.2	10.00	1,351	162.0	1.03
	38.67	g	126	1.9	32.2	3.87	522.4	62.64	0.40
	0.33	c							
slices	100.00	g	39	0.9	9.5	0.00	190.0	20.00	0.25
	154.00	g	60	1.4	14.7	0.00	292.6	30.80	0.39
	1.00	c							
nectar, canned	100.00	g	49	0.1	11.6	11.00	30.00	3.00	0.57
	249.00	g	122	0.3	28.9	27.39	74.70	7.47	1.42
	8.00	fl oz							
pie, prepared	100.00	g	224	1.9	33.0	217.00	125.0	22.00	10.00
1/6 of 8-in. pie	117.00	g	262	2.2	38.5	253.89	146.3	25.74	11.70
	1.00	slice							
slices,	100.00	g	94	0.6	24.0	6.00	130.0	11.00	0.13
sweetened,	125.00	g	118	0.8	30.0	7.50	162.5	13.75	0.16
frozen									
	0.50	c							
halves/ slices,	100.00	g	24	0.4	6.1	3.00	99.00	10.00	0.06
canned in	122.00	g	29	0.5	7.5	3.66	120.8	12.20	0.07
water									
	0.50	c							
halves/ slices,	100.00	g	44	0.6	11.6	4.00	128.0	17.00	0.03
canned in	124.00	g	55	0.8	14.4	4.96	158.7	21.08	0.04
juice									
	0.50	c							
canned in	100.00	g	42	0.4	11.1	5.00	74.00	11.00	0.10
extra light	123.50	g	52	0.5	13.7	6.18	91.39	13.59	0.12
syrup									
	0.50	c							
canned in	100.00	g	75	0.4	20.1	4.00	85.00	9.00	0.10
heavy syrup	242.00	g	182	1.0	48.6	9.68	205.7	21.78	0.24
	1.00	c							
canned in light	100.00	g	61	0.6	15.7	7.00	87.00	10.00	0.15
syrup, drained									
fruit cocktail,	100.00	g	55	0.4	14.3	6.00	85.00	13.00	0.08
canned light									
syrup									
with solids and									
liquid									

CANTALOUPE MELON	SERVING QUANTITY	SERVING UNIT	CALORIES (kCal)	PROTEIN (g)	TOTAL CARBOHYDRATES (g)	SODIUM (mg)	POTASSIUM (mg)	PHOSPHORUS (mg)	TOTAL FAT (g)
composite,	100.00	g	31	0.7	7.5	8.22	202.4	8.67	0.20
raw	165.50	g	51	1.1	12.5	13.60	334.9	14.34	0.33
	1.00	c							
honeydew,	100.00	g	36	0.5	9.1	18.00	228.0	11.00	0.14
balls	132.75	g	48	0.7	12.1	23.90	302.7	14.60	0.19
1 slice = 125g									
	0.75	c							
Navajo	100.00	g	21	0.8	4.1	11.00	140.0	9.00	0.20
	85.05	g	18	0.7	3.5	9.36	119.1	7.65	0.17
	3.00	oz							
melon balls,	100.00	g	33	0.8	7.9	31.00	280.0	12.00	0.25
frozen,	173.00	g	57	1.5	13.7	53.63	484.4	20.76	0.43
unthawed									
	1.00	c							
BANANA									
medium, 77.8	100.00	g	89	1.1	22.8	1.00	358.0	22.00	0.33
in long	118.00	g	105	1.3	27.0	1.18	422.5	25.96	0.39
	1.00	pc/ item							
dehydrated,	100.00	g	346	3.9	88.3	3.00	1,491	74.00	1.81
powder	6.20	g	21	0.2	5.5	0.19	92.44	4.59	0.11
	1.00	tbsp							
chips, dried	100.00	g	519	2.3	58.4	6.00	536.0	56.00	14.29
	42.53	g	221	1.0	24.8	2.55	227.9	23.81	33.60
	1.50	oz							
pudding, mix	100.00	g	366	0.0	93.0	788.00	17.00	5.00	0.40
mix to make ½ c	22.00	g	81	0.0	20.5	172.36	3.74	1.10	0.09
1 package= 88g =	1.00	svg							
3 ½ oz									
pudding,	100.00	g	127	2.4	21.2	196.00	110	69.00	3.60
ready to eat									
1 can = 5 oz	142.00	g	180	3.4	30.1	278.32	156.2	97.98	5.11
	5.00	oz							

ORANGE	SERVING QUANTITY	SERVING UNIT	CALORIES (kCal)	PROTEIN (g)	TOTAL CARBOHYDRATES (g)	SODIUM (mg)	POTASSIUM (mg)	PHOSPHORUS (mg)	TOTAL FAT (g)
whole, 2-5/8"	100.00	g	47	0.9	11.8	0.00	181.0	14.00	0.12
diameter	131.00	g	62	1.2	15.4	0.00	237.1	18.34	0.16
	1.00	pc/ item							
Valencia	100.00	g	49	1.0	11.9	0.00	179.0	17.00	0.30
(California)	135.00	g	66	1.4	16.1	0.00	241.7	22.95	0.41
	0.75	c							
Navel	100.00	g	49	0.9	12.5	1.00	166.0	28.46	0.15
(California)	123.75	g	61	1.1	15.5	1.24	205.4	23.00	0.19
	0.75	c							
Clementines	100.00	g	47	0.9	12.0	1.00	177.0	21.00	0.15
	74.00	g	35	0.6	8.9	0.74	130.9	15.54	0.11
	1.00	pc/ item							
orange	100.00	g	47	0.9	11.8	0.00	181.0	14.00	0.12
sections	135.00	g	63	1.3	15.9	0.00	244.4	18.90	0.16
	0.75	c							
juice	100.00	g	45	0.7	10.4	1.00	200.0	17.00	0.20
	248.00	g	112	1.7	25.8	2.48	496.0	42.16	0.50
	8.00	fl oz							
Florida, sections	100.00	g	46	0.7	11.5	0.00	169.0	12.00	0.21
1 fruit = 141g	138.75	g	64	1.0	16.0	0.00	234.5	16.65	0.29
	0.75	c							
soda	100.00	g	48	0.0	12.3	12.00	2.00	1.00	0.00
	248.00	g	119	0.0	30.5	29.76	4.96	2.48	0.00
	8.00	fl oz							
marmalade	100.00	g	246	0.3	66.3	56.00	37.00	4.00	0.00
	20.00	g	49	0.1	13.3	11.20	7.40	0.80	0.00
	1.00	tbsp							
juice, frozen	100.00	g	95	0.5	23.2	8.00	100.0	13.00	0.00
	238.40	g	70	0.4	17.2	5.92	74.00	9.62	0.00
	1.00	c							
orange peel	100.00	g	97	1.5	25.0	3.00	212.0	21.00	0.20
zest	2.00	g	2	0.0	0.5	0.06	4.24	0.42	0.00
	1.00	tsp							
juice,	100.00	g	47	0.7	11.0	4.00	184.0	17.00	0.15
unsweetened,	249.00	g	117	1.7	27.4	9.96	458.2	42.33	0.37
canned	8.00	fl oz							
Mandarin,	100.00	g	37	0.6	9.6	5.00	133.0	10.00	
canned in juice	249.00	g	92	1.5	23.8	12.45	331.2	24.90	
	1.00	c							
juice, light, no	100.00	g	21	0.2	5.4	4.00	188.0	4.00	
pulp	240.00	g	50	0.5	13.0	9.60	451.2	9.60	
	8.00	fl oz							
Mandarin,	100.00	g	61	0.5	16.2	6.00	78.00	10.00	
canned in light	252.00	g	154	1.1	40.8	15.12	196.6	25.20	
syrup	1.00	c							

46

LEMON

	SERVING QUANTITY	SERVING UNIT	CALORIES (kCal)	PROTEIN (g)	TOTAL CARBOHYDRATES (g)	SODIUM (mg)	POTASSIUM (mg)	PHOSPHORUS (mg)	TOTAL FAT (g)
whole, without seeds	100	g	20	1.2	10.7	3.00	145.0	15.00	0.30
	108.00	g	22	1.3	11.6	3.24	156.6	16.20	0.32
	1.00	pc/ item							
peeled, 2-1/8" in diameter)	100.00	g	29	1.1	9.3	2.00	138.0	16.00	0.30
	58.00	g	17	0.6	5.4	1.16	80.04	9.28	0.17
	1.00	pc/ item							
juice, fresh	100.00	g	22	0.4	6.9	1.00	103.0	8.00	0.24
	30.50	g	7	0.1	2.1	0.31	31.42	2.44	0.07
	1.00	fl oz							
peel or zest	100.00	g	47	1.5	16.0	6.00	160.0	12.00	0.30
	2.00	g	1	0.0	0.3	0.12	3.20	0.24	0.01
	1.00	tsp							
pudding mix 1 svg = ½ c 1 package = 85g	100.00	g	363	0.1	91.8	506.00	5.00	3.00	0.50
	21.20	g	77	0.0	19.5	107.27	1.06	0.64	0.11
	1.00	svg							
juice, canned	100.00	g	17	0.5	5.6	24.00	109.0	9.00	0.07
	30.50	g	5	0.1	1.7	7.32	33.25	2.75	0.02
	1.00	fl oz							
soda, lemon lime	100.00	g	40	0.1	24.9	9.00	1.00	0.00	0.02
	245.60	g	98	0.1	10.1	22.10	2.46	0.00	0.05
	8.00	fl oz							
juice, unsweetened, frozen	100.00	g	22	0.5	6.5	1.00	89.00	8.00	0.32
	5.08	g	1	0.0	0.3	0.05	4.52	0.41	0.02
	1.00	tsp							
pudding, ready to eat 1 can= 5 oz	100.00	g	125	0.1	25.0	140.00	1.00	5.00	3.00
	142.00	g	178	0.1	35.5	198.80	1.42	7.10	4.26
	1.00	can/ item							
tea, black, sweetened, ready to drink	100.00	g	45	0.0	10.8	3.00	14.00	1.00	0.22
	271.00	g	122	0.0	29.3	8.13	37.94	2.71	0.60
	1.00	c							

	SERVING QUANTITY	SERVING UNIT	CALORIES (kCal)	PROTEIN (g)	TOTAL CARBOHYDRATES (g)	SODIUM (mg)	POTASSIUM (mg)	PHOSPHORUS (mg)	TOTAL FAT (g)
LIME									
whole, 2" in diameter	100.00	g	30	0.7	10.5	2.00	102.0	18.00	0.20
	67.00	g	20	0.5	7.1	1.34	68.34	12.06	0.13
	1.00	pc/ item							
juice, fresh	100.00	g	25	0.4	8.4	2.00	117.0	14.00	0.07
	5.13	g	1	0.0	0.4	0.10	6.01	0.72	0.00
	1.00	tsp							
juice, unsweetened, canned	100.00	g	21	0.3	6.7	16.00	75.00	10.00	0.23
	246.00	g	52	0.6	16.5	39.36	184.5	24.60	0.57
	1.00	c							
frozen ice dessert	100.00	g	128	0.4	32.6	22.00	3.00	1.00	0.00
	99.00	g	127	0.4	32.3	21.78	2.97	0.99	0.00
	0.50	c							
LYCHEE									
whole, fresh	100.00	g	66	0.8	16.5	1.00	171.0	31.00	0.44
	142.50	g	94	1.2	23.6	1.43	243.7	44.18	0.63
	0.75	c							
dried	100.00	g	277	3.8	70.7	3.00	1,110	181.00	1.20
	40.00	g	111	1.5	28.3	1.20	444.0	72.40	0.48
	16.00	pcs/ items							
MANGO									
whole, fresh	100.00	g	60	0.8	15.0	1.00	168.0	14.00	0.38
	207.00	g	124	1.7	31.0	2.07	347.8	28.98	0.79
	1.00	pc/ item							
dired, sweetened	100.00	g	319	2.5	78.6	162.00	279.0	50.00	1.18
nectar, canned	100.00	g	51	0.1	13.1	5.00	24.00	2.00	0.06
	251.00	g	128	0.3	32.9	12.55	60.24	5.02	0.15
	1.00	c							

	SERVING QUANTITY	SERVING UNIT	CALORIES (kCal)	PROTEIN (g)	TOTAL CARBOHYDRATES (g)	SODIUM (mg)	POTASSIUM (mg)	PHOSPHORUS (mg)	TOTAL FAT (g)
APRICOT									
whole, fresh	100.00	g	48	1.4	11.1	1.00	259.0	23.00	0.39
	140.00	g	67	2.0	15.6	1.40	362.6	32.20	0.55
	4.00	pcs/ items							
jam or preserves	100.00	g	242	0.7	64.4	40.00	77.00	3.00	0.20
1 packet = 0.5 oz = 14g	20.00	g	48	0.1	12.9	8.00	15.40	0.60	0.04
	1.00	tbsp							
nectar, canned	100.00	g	56	0.2	13.6	8.00	67.00	5.00	0.45
	251.00	g	141	0.4	34.2	20.08	168.2	12.55	1.13
	8.00	fl oz							
sweetened, frozen	100.00	g	98	0.7	25.1	4.00	229.0	19.00	0.10
	242.00	g	237	1.7	60.7	9.68	554.2	45.98	0.24
	1.00	c							
dehydrated, sulfured	100.00	g	320	4.9	82.9	13.00	1,850	157.00	0.62
	30.00	g	96	1.5	24.9	3.90	555.0	47.10	0.19
	0.25	c							
dried, halves, sulfured	100.00	g	241	3.4	62.6	10.00	1,162	71.00	0.51
	43.33	g	104	1.5	27.1	4.33	503.5	30.77	0.22
	0.33	c							
halves w/ skin, canned in juice	100.00	g	48	0.6	12.3	4.00	165.0	20.00	0.04
	244.00	g	117	1.5	30.1	9.76	402.6	48.80	0.10
	1.00	c							
halves with skin, canned in light syrup	100.00	g	63	0.5	16.5	4.00	138.0	32.89	0.05
	253.00	g	159	1.3	41.7	10.12	349.1	13.00	0.13
	1.00	c							
PLUM									
whole, fresh, sliced	100.00	g	46	0.7	11.4	0.00	157.0	16.00	0.28
	165.00	g	76	1.2	18.8	0.00	259.1	26.40	0.46
	1.00	c							
sauce	100.00	g	184	0.9	42.8	538.00	259.0	22.00	1.04
	19.00	g	35	0.2	8.1	102.22	49.21	4.18	0.20
	1.00	tbsp							
purple, pitted, canned in water	100.00	g	41	0.4	11.0	1.00	126.0	13.00	0.01
	249.00	g	102	1.0	27.5	2.49	313.7	32.37	0.02
	1.00	c							
purple, canned in juice	100.00	g	58	0.5	15.2	1.00	154.0	15.00	0.02
	252.00	g	146	1.3	38.2	2.52	388.1	37.80	0.05
	1.00	c							

PRUNE

	SERVING QUANTITY	SERVING UNIT	CALORIES (kCal)	PROTEIN (g)	TOTAL CARBOHYDRATES (g)	SODIUM (mg)	POTASSIUM (mg)	PHOSPHORUS (mg)	TOTAL FAT (g)
puree	100.00	g	257	2.1	65.1	23.00	852.00	72.00	0.20
	28.35	g	73	0.6	18.5	6.52	241.54	20.41	0.06
	1.00	oz							
dried	100.00	g	240	2.2	63.9	2.00	732.00	69.00	0.38
	42.50	g	102	0.9	27.2	0.85	311.10	29.33	0.16
	0.25	c							
juice, canned	100.00	g	71	0.6	17.5	4.00	276.00	25.00	0.03
	256.00	g	182	1.6	44.7	10.24	706.56	64.00	0.08
	8.00	fl oz							
dehydrated, stewed	100.00	g	113	1.2	29.7	2.00	353.00	37.00	0.24
	36.40	g	41	0.5	10.8	0.73	128.49	13.47	0.09
	0.13	c							
dehydrated, low moisture	100.00	g	339	3.7	89.1	5.00	1,058	112.00	0.73
	33.00	g	112	1.2	29.4	1.65	349.14	36.96	0.24
	0.25	c							

RHUBARB

	SERVING QUANTITY	SERVING UNIT	CALORIES (kCal)	PROTEIN (g)	TOTAL CARBOHYDRATES (g)	SODIUM (mg)	POTASSIUM (mg)	PHOSPHORUS (mg)	TOTAL FAT (g)
whole, fresh, diced	100.00	g	21	0.9	4.5	4.00	288.00	14.00	0.20
	81.33	g	17	0.7	3.7	3.25	234.24	11.39	0.16
	0.67	c							
diced, frozen	100.00	g	21	0.6	5.1	2.00	108.00	12.00	0.11
	137.00	g	29	0.8	7.0	2.74	147.96	16.44	0.15
	1.00	c							
frozen, cooked with sugar	100.00	g	116	0.4	31.2	1.00	96.00	8.00	0.05
	120.00	g	139	0.5	37.4	1.20	115.20	9.60	0.06
	0.50	c							

POMEGRANATE

	SERVING QUANTITY	SERVING UNIT	CALORIES (kCal)	PROTEIN (g)	TOTAL CARBOHYDRATES (g)	SODIUM (mg)	POTASSIUM (mg)	PHOSPHORUS (mg)	TOTAL FAT (g)
whole, fresh, 4" in diameter	100.00	g	83	1.7	18.7	3.00	236.00	36.00	1.17
	282.00	g	234	4.7	52.7	8.46	665.52	101.52	3.30
	1.00	pc/ item							
juice, bottled	100.00	g	54	0.2	13.1	9.00	214.00	11.00	0.29
	251.20	g	136	0.4	33.0	22.61	537.57	27.63	0.73
	8.00	fl oz							

	SERVING QUANTITY	SERVING UNIT	CALORIES (Kcal)	PROTEIN (g)	TOTAL CARBOHYDRATES (g)	SODIUM (mg)	POTASSIUM (mg)	PHOSPHORUS (mg)	TOTAL FAT (g)
PAPAYA									
whole, fresh, cubes	100.00	g	43	0.5	10.8	8.00	182.00	10.00	0.26
	140.00	g	60	0.7	15.2	11.20	254.80	14.00	0.36
	1.00	c							
nectar, canned	100.00	g	57	0.2	14.5	5.00	31.00	0.00	0.15
	250.00	g	143	0.4	36.3	12.50	77.50	0.00	0.38
	8.00	fl oz							
canned with heavy syrup, drained	100.00	g	206	0.1	55.8	9.00	67.00	6.00	0.55
	39.00	g	80	0.1	21.8	3.51	26.13	2.34	0.21
	1.00	pc/ chunk							
NECTARINE									
whole, fresh, slices	100.00	g	44	1.1	10.6	0.00	201.00	26.00	0.32
	138.00	g	61	1.5	14.7	0.00	277.38	35.88	0.44
	1.00	c							
PERSIMMON									
whole, fresh	100.00	g	127	0.8	33.5	1.00	310.00	26.00	0.40
	25.00	g	32	0.2	8.4	0.25	77.50	6.50	0.10
	1.00	pc/ item							
Japanese, fresh, 2-1/2" in diameter	100.00	g	70	0.6	18.6	1.00	161.00	17.00	0.19
	168.00	g	118	1.0	31.2	1.68	270.48	28.56	0.32
	1.00	pc/item							
Japanese, dried	100.00	g	274	1.4	73.4	2.00	802.00	81.00	0.59
	34.00	g	93	0.5	25.0	0.68	272.68	27.54	0.20
	1.00	pc/ item							
PURPLE PASSION FRUIT/ GRANADILLA									
whole, fresh – no refuse	100.00	g	97	2.2	23.4	28.00	348.00	68.00	0.70
	18.00	g	18	0.4	4.2	5.04	62.60	12.20	0.13
	1.00	pc/ fruit							
nectar, no ice	100.00	g	67	1.2	17.4	4.00	112.00	5.00	0.06
	31.00	g	21	0.1	5.4	1.24	34.70	1.55	0.02
	1.00	fl oz							
juice, purple passion fruit	100.00	g	51	0.4	13.6	6.00	278.00	13.00	0.05
	30.90	g	16	0.1	4.2	1.85	85.90	4.02	0.02
	1.00	fl oz							
juice, yellow passion fruit	100.00	g	60	0.7	14.5	6.00	278.00	25.00	0.18
	30.90	g	19	0.2	4.5	1.85	85.90	7.72	0.06
	1.00	fl oz							

WATER MELON	SERVING QUANTITY	SERVING UNIT	CALORIES (kCal)	PROTEIN (g)	TOTAL CARBOHYDRATES (g)	SODIUM (mg)	POTASSIUM (mg)	PHOSPHORUS (mg)	TOTAL FAT (g)
raw, balls	100.00	g	30	0.6	7.6	1.00	112.00	11.00	0.15
	154.00	g	46	0.9	11.6	1.54	172.00	16.00	0.23
	1.00	c							
juice, 100%,	100.00	g	30	0.6	7.6	1.00	112.00	11.00	0.15
no ice	30.00	g	9	0.2	2.3	0.30	33.60	3.30	0.05
	1.00	fl oz							
seeds, kernels,	100.00	g	557	28.3	15.3	99.00	648.00	755.0	47.37
dried	28.35	g	158	8.0	4.3	28.10	184.00	214.0	13.40
	1.00	oz							
FIG									
raw	100.00	g	74	0.8	19.2	1.00	232.00	14.00	0.30
	50.00	g	37	0.4	9.6	0.50	116.00	7.00	0.15
	1.00	pc/ item							
dried	100.00	g	249	3.3	63.9	10.00	680.00	67.00	0.92
	8.00	g	20	0.3	5.1	0.80	54.40	5.36	0.07
	1.00	pc							
canned	100.00	g	75	0.6	19.4	1.00	157.00	10.00	0.24
	250.00	g	188	1.4	48.4	2.50	392.00	25.00	0.60
	1.00	c							
dried, stewed	100.00	g	107	1.4	27.6	4.00	294.00	29.00	0.40
	259.00	g	277	3.7	71.4	10.40	761.00	75.10	1.04
	1.00	c							
canned, water pack, solids/liquids	100.00	g	53	0.4	14.0	1.00	103.00	10.00	0.10
	248.00	g	131	1.0	34.7	2.48	255.00	24.80	0.25
	1.00	c							
canned, light syrup pack, solids/liquids	100.00	g	69	0.4	18.0	1.00	102.00	10.00	0.10
	252.00	g	174	1.0	45.2	2.52	257.00	25.20	0.25
	1.00	c							
GUAVA									
raw	100.00	g	68	2.6	14.3	2.00	417.00	40.00	0.95
	55.00	g	37	1.4	7.9	1.10	229.00	22.00	0.52
	1.00	pc/ item							
nectar	100.00	g	48	0.3	13.3	6.00	33.00	3.00	0.07
no ice	31.00	g	15	0.1	4.1	1.86	10.20	0.93	0.02
	1.00	fl oz							
paste	100.00	g	280	0.1	77.6	2.00	69.00	3.00	0.27
	20.00	g	56	0.0	14.5	0.40	13.80	0.60	0.05
	1.00	tbsp							

	SERVING QUANTITY	SERVING UNIT	CALORIES (KCal)	PROTEIN (g)	TOTAL CARBOHYDRATES (g)	SODIUM (mg)	POTASSIUM (mg)	PHOSPHORUS (mg)	TOTAL FAT (g)
DATES									
whole, dried	100.00	g	282	2.5	75.0	2.00	656.0	62.00	0.39
	8.00	g	23	0.2	6.0	0.16	52.50	4.96	0.03
	1.00	pc/ item							
Medjool,	100.00	g	277	1.8	75.0	1.00	696.0	62.00	0.15
pitted	24.00	g	67	0.4	18.0	0.24	167.0	14.90	0.04
	1.00	pc/item							
candy	100.00	g	379	4.2	58.1	22.00	540.0	117.0	18.04
	28.35	g	107	1.2	16.5	6.24	153.0	33.20	5.11
	1.00	oz							
POMELO									
whole, fresh	100.00	g	38	0.8	9.6	1.00	216.0	17.00	0.04
section	190.00	g	72	1.4	18.3	1.90	410.0	32.30	0.08
	1.00	c							
MANGOSTEEN									
canned,	100.00	g	73	0.4	17.9	7.00	48.00	8.00	0.58
syrup pack									
drained	196.00	g	143	0.8	35.1	13.70	94.10	15.70	1.14
	1.00	c							
JACKFRUIT									
raw, fresh	100.00	g	95	1.7	23.3	2.00	448.0	21.00	0.64
slices	165.00	g	157	2.8	38.4	3.30	739.0	34.60	1.06
	1.00	c							
canned,	100.00	g	92	0.4	23.9	11.00	96.00	6.00	0.14
syrup pack									
drained	178.00	g	164	0.6	42.6	19.60	171.0	10.70	0.25
	1.00	c							
DURIAN									
raw or frozen	100.00	g	147	1.5	27.1	2.00	436.0	39.00	5.33
chopped or	243.00	g	357	3.6	65.8	4.86	1,060	94.80	13.00
diced									
	1.00	c							
SOURSOP									
raw, pulp	100.00	g	66	1.0	16.8	14.00	278.0	27.00	0.30
	225.00	g	148	2.3	37.9	31.50	626.0	60.80	0.68
	1.00	c							
nectar	100.00	g	59	0.1	14.9	8.00	25.00	2.00	0.17
no ice, pure	31.00	g	18	0.0	4.6	2.48	7.75	0.62	0.05
	1.00	fl oz							

PLANTAIN	SERVING QUANTITY	SERVING UNIT	CALORIES (Kcal)	PROTEIN (g)	TOTAL CARBOHYDRATES (g)	SODIUM (mg)	POTASSIUM (mg)	PHOSPHORUS (mg)	TOTAL FAT (g)
ripe, raw, fresh	100.00	g	122	1.3	31.9	4.00	487.00	32.00	0.35
	180.00	g	220	2.3	57.4	7.20	877.00	57.60	0.63
	1.00	pc/ item							
green, raw, fresh	100.00	g	152	1.3	36.7	2.00	431.00	31.00	0.07
	267.00	g	406	3.3	97.9	5.34	1,150.0	82.80	0.19
	1.00	pc/item							
green, boiled	100.00	g	121	1.1	29.2	2.00	289.00	24.00	0.08
	137.00	g	166	1.5	39.9	2.74	396.00	32.90	0.11
	1.00	c							
green, fried	100.00	g	309	1.5	49.2	2.00	482.00	44.00	11.81
	118.00	g	365	1.8	58.0	2.36	569.00	51.90	13.90
	1.00	c							
yellow, raw, fresh	100.00	g	122	1.3	31.9	4.00	487.00	32.00	0.35
	270.00	g	329	3.5	86.1	10.8	1,310.0	86.40	0.95
	1.00	pc/ item							
yellow, baked	100.00	g	155	1.5	41.4	2.00	477.00	37.00	0.16
	139.00	g	215	2.1	57.5	2.78	663.00	51.40	0.22
	1.00	c							
chips	100.00	g	531	2.3	63.8	202	786.00	78.00	29.59
	28.35	g	151	0.6	18.1	57.3	223.00	22.10	8.39
	1.00	oz							
AVOCADO									
fresh, raw	100.00	g	160	2.0	8.5	7.00	485.00	52.00	14.66
mashed/ pureed	230.00	g	368	4.6	19.6	16.1	1,120.0	120.0	33.70
	1.00	c							
oil	100.00	g	884	0.0	0.0	0.00	0.00	0.00	100.00
	14.00	g	124	0.0	0.0	0.00	0.00	0.00	14.00
	1.00	tbsp							
dressing	100.00	g	427	1.9	7.4	867	58.00	31.00	43.33
	15.30	g	65	0.3	1.1	133.	8.87	4.74	6.63
	1.00	tbsp							
California, raw/fresh	100.00	g	167	2.0	8.6	8.00	507.00	54.00	15.41
no seed and skin	136.00	g	227	2.7	11.8	10.9	690.00	73.40	21.00
	1.00	pc/ item							
Florida, fresh/ raw no seed and skin	100.00	g	120	2.2	7.8	2.00	351.00	40.00	10.06
	304.00	g	365	6.8	23.8	6.08	1,070.0	122.0	30.60
	1.00	pc/ item							
Guacamole	100.00	g	155	2.0	8.5	344	472.00	51.00	14.18
	15.00	G	23	0.3	1.3	51.6	70.80	7.65	2.13
	1.00	tbsp							

	SERVING QUANTITY	SERVING UNIT	CALORIES (kCal)	PROTEIN (g)	TOTAL CARBOHYDRATES (g)	SODIUM (mg)	POTASSIUM (mg)	PHOSPHORUS (mg)	TOTAL FAT (g)
TAMARIND									
fresh, raw	100.00	g	239	2.8	62.5	28.00	628	113	0.60
	2.00	g	5	0.1	1.3	0.56	12.60	2.26	0.01
	1.00	pc/item							
candy	100.00	g	331	0.0	92.0	1,643	309.0	56.00	0.00
	22.00	g	73	0.0	20.2	361.00	68.00	12.30	0.00
	1.00	tbsp							
dried	100.00	g	254	2.5	66.2	25.00	565	102	0.57
	160.00	g	406	4.0	106	40.00	904	163	0.91
	1.00	c							
SAPODILLA									
fresh/raw	100.00	g	83	0.4	20.0	12.00	193	12.00	1.10
	170.00	g	141	0.8	33.9	20.40	328	20.40	1.87
	1.00	pc/ item							
SUGARAPPLE *(Sweetsop)*									
fresh, raw (2-7/8" in diameter)	100.00	g	94	2.1	23.6	9.00	247	32.00	0.29
	155.00	g	146	3.2	36.6	14.00	383	49.60	0.45
	1.00	pc/ item							
STARFRUIT									
fresh/ raw	100.00	g	31	1.0	6.7	2.00	133	12.00	0.33
	90.00	g	28	0.9	6.1	1.80	120.0	10.80	0.30
	1.00	pc/ item							

D. Carbohydrates

(Grains, Breads, Pasta/Noodles, Cereals)

Hey there!

Do you need to print out this Food List?

You can download a printable version of this chart by scanning the QR code below or copying the link on your computer browser.

https://go.renaltracker.com/printfoodlist

BREADS

	SERVING QUANTITY	SERVING UNIT	CALORIES (kCal)	PROTEIN (g)	TOTAL CARBOHYDRATES (g)	SODIUM (mg)	POTASSIUM (mg)	PHOSPHORUS (mg)	TOTAL FAT (g)
whole wheat	100.00	g	252	12.5	42.7	455.0	254	212.0	3.50
	50.00	g	126	6.2	21.4	227.5	127.0	106.0	1.75
	2.00	slices							
white	100.00	g	266	8.9	49.4	490.0	126.0	98.00	490.00
	50.00	g	133	4.4	24.7	245.0	63.00	49.00	245.00
	2.00	slices							
french, small (2'x2.5'x1.75')	100.00	g	272	10.8	51.9	602.0	117.0	105.0	2.42
	32.00	g	87	3.4	16.6	192.6	37.44	33.60	0.77
	1.00	slice							
pita, 6.5"	100.00	g	275	9.1	55.7	536.0	120.0	97.00	1.20
	60.00	g	165	5.5	33.4	321.6	72.00	58.20	0.72
	1.00	pc							
sourdough	100.00	g	272	10.8	51.9	602.0	117.0	105.0	2.42
	50.00	g	136	5.4	25.9	301.0	58.50	52.50	1.21
	2.00	slices							
rye	100.00	g	259	8.5	48.3	603.0	166.0	125.0	33.00
	32.00	g	83	2.7	15.5	192.9	53.12	40.00	1.06
	1.00	slice							
bagels, wheat	100.00	g	250	10.2	48.9	439.0	165.0	142.0	1.53
	105.00	g	262	10.7	51.3	461.0	173.0	149.0	1.61
	1.00	reg pc							
biscuits	100.00	g	362	7.5	43.9	930.0	184.0	501.0	18.19
	45.00	g	163	3.4	19.8	418.0	82.80	225.0	8.19
	1.00	pc							
sprouted, wheat	100.00	g	188	13.2	33.9	474.0	198.0	176.0	0.00
	26.00	g	49	3.4	8.8	123.0	51.50	45.80	0.00
	1.00	slice							
cracked, wheat	100.00	g	274	10.7	47.5	473.0	141.0	129.0	4.53
	28.00	g	77	3.0	13.3	132.0	39.50	36.10	1.27
	1.00	reg slice							
tortillas, corn ready-to-bake or fry	100.00	g	218	5.7	44.6	45.00	186.0	314.0	2.85
	24.00	g	52	1.4	10.7	10.80	44.60	75.40	0.68
	1.00	Pc							
tortillas, flour *approx. 6" diameter* ready-to-bake or fry, refrigerated	100.00	g	306	8.2	49.4	736.0	125.0	206.0	7.99
	30.00	g	92	2.5	14.8	221.0	37.50	61.80	2.40
	1.00	pc							

BREADS

	SERVING QUANTITY	SERVING UNIT	CALORIES (kcal)	PROTEIN (g)	TOTAL CARBOHYDRATES (g)	SODIUM (mg)	POTASSIUM (mg)	PHOSPHORUS (mg)	TOTAL FAT (g)
tortilla, whole wheat ready-to-bake or fry	100.00	g	310	9.8	45.9	617.00	262.0	346.0	9.76
	41.00	g	127	4.0	18.8	253.00	107.0	142.0	4.00
	1.00	pc							
ciabatta (yeast bread) italian, grecian, aarmenian thick sllice	100.00	g	259	9.5	48.1	618.00	124.0	95.00	2.73
	43.00	g	111	4.1	20.7	266.00	53.30	40.80	1.17
	1.00	pc							
focaccia, plain (Italian flatbread)	100.00	g	249	8.8	35.8	561.00	114.0	128.0	7.89
	57.00	g	142	5.0	20.4	320.00	65.00	73.00	4.50
	1.00	pc							
Pita, medium	100.00	g	275	9.1	55.7	536.00	120.0	97.00	1.20
	57.00	g	157	5.2	31.7	306.00	68.40	55.30	0.68
	1.00	pc							
Naan, plain	100.00	g	291	9.6	50.4	465.00	125.0	100.0	5.65
	90.00	g	262	8.7	45.4	418.00	112.0	90.00	5.08
	1.00	pc							
Paratha, whole wheat, frozen	100.00	g	326	6.4	45.4	467.00	185.0	188.0	6.70
	79.00	g	258	5.0	35.9	495.00	196.0	199.0	7.10
	1.00	pc							
brioche	100.00	g	418	8.8	35.8	452.00	139.0	120.0	13.20
	77.00	g	322	6.7	27.6	357.00	110.0	94.80	10.40
	1.00	pc							
croissants, plain medium	100.00	g	406	8.2	45.8	440.00	120.0	125.0	26.80
	57.00	g	231	4.7	26.1	339.00	92.40	96.20	20.60
	1.00	pc							
croissants, chocolate	100.00	g	421	7.4	49.4	384.00	118.0	105.0	21.00
	57.00	g	240	4.2	28.2	219.00	67.30	59.80	12.00
	1.00	pc							
croissants, cheese	100.00	g	414	9.2	47.0	361.00	132.0	130.0	20.90
	57.00	g	236	5.2	26.8	206.00	75.22	74.10	11.90
	1.00	pc							
muffins, english, whole grain white	100.00	g	245	7.0	50.2	386.00	130.0	127.0	1.75
	57.00	g	140	4.0	28.6	220.00	74.10	72.40	1.00
	1.00	pc							
muffins, english, whole wheat	100.00	g	203	8.8	40.4	364.00	210.0	282.0	2.10
	66.00	g	134	5.8	26.7	240.00	139.0	186.0	1.39
	1.00	pc							

58

BREADS

	SERVING QUANTITY	SERVING UNIT	CALORIES (kCal)	PROTEIN (g)	TOTAL CARBOHYDRATES (g)	SODIUM (mg)	POTASSIUM (mg)	PHOSPHORUS (mg)	TOTAL FAT (g)
muffins, english, mixed-grain includes granola	100.00	g	235	9.1	46.3	298.00	156.0	81.00	1.80
	66.00	g	155	6.0	30.6	197.00	103.0	53.40	1.19
	1.00	pc							
pumpernickle, med or regular slice	100.00	g	250	8.7	47.5	596.00	208.0	178.0	3.10
	32.00	g	80	2.8	15.2	191.00	66.60	57.00	0.99
	1.00	pc							
cinammon, medium or regular slice	100.00	g	253	7.1	44.4	388.00	74.00	57.00	5.29
	28.00	g	71	2.0	12.4	109.00	20.70	16.00	1.48
	1.00	pc							
raisin, med or regular slice	100.00	g	273	8.8	52.2	432.00	180.0	112.0	3.26
	28.00	g	76	2.5	14.6	121.00	50.40	31.40	0.91
	1.00	pc							
roll, multigrain med, reg, sandwich size	100.00	g	263	9.6	44.6	458.00	160.0	122.0	6.00
	43.00	g	113	4.1	19.2	197.00	68.80	52.50	2.58
	1.00	pc							
bread stuffing, homemade dry mix, prepared	100.00	g	177	3.1	21.7	471.00	72.00	41.00	8.51
	228.00	g	404	7.2	49.5	1,070	164.0	93.50	19.40
	1.00	pc							

GRITS

	SERVING QUANTITY	SERVING UNIT	CALORIES (kCal)	PROTEIN (g)	TOTAL CARBOHYDRATES (g)	SODIUM (mg)	POTASSIUM (mg)	PHOSPHORUS (mg)	TOTAL FAT (g)
corn, yellow, quick, unenriched cooked with water, no salt	100.00	g	59	1.4	12.9	2.00	21.00	11.00	0.19
	242.00	g	143	3.4	31.2	4.84	50.82	26.62	0.46
	1.00	c							
corn, white, quick, unenriched cooked with water	100.00	g	59	1.4	12.9	2.00	21.00	11.00	0.19
	242.00	g	143	3.4	31.2	4.84	50.82	26.62	0.46
	1.00	c							
POLENTA (cornmeal)	100.00	g							
	240.00	g	139	2.7	30.	170.00	50.40	36.00	0.67
	1	c							

PASTA

PASTA	SERVING QUANTITY	SERVING UNIT	CALORIES (kcal)	PROTEIN (g)	TOTAL CARBOHYDRATES (g)	SODIUM (mg)	POTASSIUM (mg)	PHOSPHORUS (mg)	TOTAL FAT (g)
spaghetti, unenriched, cooked	100.00	g	158	5.8	30.9	1.00	44.00	58.00	0.93
	70.00	g	111	4.1	21.6	0.70	30.80	40.60	0.65
	0.50	c							
spaghetti, enriched, cooked	100.00	g	158	5.8	30.9	1.00	44.00	58.00	0.93
	140.00	g	221	8.1	43.2	1.40	61.60	81.20	1.30
	1.00	c							
spaghetti, whole wheat, cooked	100.00	g	149	6.0	30.1	4.00	96.00	127.0	1.71
	140.00	g	209	8.4	42.1	5.60	134.4	177.8	2.39
	1.00	c							
bowtie/farfalle, enriched, cooked	100.00	g	136	4.8	27.4	1.10	24.51	-na-	0.55
	154.79	g	210	7.4	42.3	0.16	37.93	-na-	0.86
	1.00	c							
fusilli, enriched, cooked	100.00	g	161	5.7	32.5	1.30	29.09	-na-	0.66
	130.41	g	210	7.4	42.3	1.70	37.93	-na-	0.86
	1.00	c							
penne, enriched, cooked	100.00	g	169	6.0	34.1	1.37	30.55	-na-	0.69
	124.17	g	210	7.4	42.3	1.70	37.93	-na-	0.86
	1.00	c							
macaroni, enriched, cooked	100.00	g	133	4.7	26.8	1.08	24.04	-na-	0.54
	157.79	g	210	7.4	42.3	1.70	37.93	-na-	0.86
	1.00	c							
lasagna, enriched, boiled/drained	100.00	g	150	5.3	30.1	1.21	26.98	-na-	0.61
	140.62	g	210	7.4	42.3	1.70	37.93	-na-	0.86
	1.00	c							
whole grain, 51%whole wheat	100.00	g	156	5.7	30.9	4.00	71.00	97.00	1.48

rest enriched semolina, cooked spaghetti, unenriched, cooked

CRACKERS

	SERVING QUANTITY	SERVING UNIT	CALORIES (kcal)	PROTEIN (g)	TOTAL CARBOHYDRATES (g)	SODIUM (mg)	POTASSIUM (mg)	PHOSPHORUS (mg)	TOTAL FAT (g)
melba toast, rye 3 3/4" x 1 3/4" x 1/8"	100.00	g	389	11.6	77.3	899.00	193.0	183.0	3.40
	15.00	g	58	1.7	11.6	134.85	28.95	27.45	0.51
	3.00	pcs							
melba toast, wheat	100.00	g	374	12.9	76.4	837.00	148.0	165.0	2.30
	15.00	g	56	1.9	11.5	125.55	22.20	24.75	0.35
	3.00	pcs							
saltine, low salt (square)	100.00	g	421	9.5	74.3	198.00	724.0	111.0	8.85
	15.00	g	63	1.4	11.2	29.70	108.6	16.65	1.33
	5.00	pcs							
saltine, fat-free, low sodium	100.00	g	393	10.5	82.3	849.00	115.0	113.0	1.60
	15.00	g	59	1.6	12.4	127.35	17.25	16.95	0.24
	3.00	pcs							
saltines, whole wheat/multi-grain	100.00	g	398	7.1	68.3	1,214	221.0	196.0	10.71
	14.00	g	56	1.0	9.6	169.96	30.94	27.44	1.50
	1.00	svg							
whole wheat, low salt	100.00	g	443	8.8	68.6	186.00	297.0	295.0	17.20
	28.00	g	124	2.5	19.2	52.08	83.16	82.60	4.82
	7.00	pcs							
whole wheat, reduced fat 1 svg= 29g	100.00	g	416	11.3	75.5	745.00	373.0	364.0	7.59
	4.20	g	17	0.5	3.2	31.29	15.67	15.29	0.32
	1.00	pcs							
graham, plain or honey, low fat	100.00	g	386	5.7	78.0	629.00	171.0	163.0	5.71
	35.00	g	135	2.0	27.3	220.15	59.85	57.05	2.00
	1.00	svg							
goldfish (fish-shaped), flavored	100.00	g	463	10.2	65.7	970.00	224.0	167.0	17.71
	5.20	g	24	0.5	3.4	50.44	11.65	8.68	0.92
	10.00	pcs							
toast thins, low sodium	100.00	g	442	6.5	67.7	177.00	306.0	266.0	16.13
	31.00	g	137	2.0	21.0	54.87	94.86	82.46	5.00
	1.00	svg							

RICE

	SERVING QUANTITY	SERVING UNIT	CALORIES (kcal)	PROTEIN (g)	TOTAL CARBOHYDRATES (g)	SODIUM (mg)	POTASSIUM (mg)	PHOSPHORUS (mg)	TOTAL FAT (g)
white, unenriched	100.00	g	359	6.9	79.8	5.00	75.00	94.00	1.30
white, cooked, glutinous	100.00	g	96	2.0	21.0	5.00	20.00	33.00	0.27
	174.00	g	167	3.5	36.5	6.60	26.40	43.60	0.36
	1.00	c							
white, long-grain, parboiled enriched, cooked	100.00	g	123	2.9	26.1	0.00	29.00	37.00	0.21
	158.00	g	194	4.6	41.2	0.00	53.90	68.80	0.39
	1.00	c							
flour, white, unenriched	100.00	g	359	6.9	79.8	0.00	26.00	33.00	0.19
						0.00	53.30	67.60	0.39
white, steamed, Chinese restaurant	100.00	g	151	3.2	33.9				
cup, loosely packed	132.00	g	199	4.2	44.7	1.00	265.0	319.0	3.85
	1.00	c							
white, medium-grain, cooked unenriched	100.00	g	130	2.4	28.6	201.00	86.00	102.00	0.96
	186.00	g	242	4.4	53.2	394.00	169.0	200.0	1.88
	1.00	c							
white, short-grain, cooked unenriched	100.00	g	130	2.4	28.7	3.00	101.0	82.00	0.34
	205.00	g	266	4.8	58.8	4.92	166.0	134.0	0.56
	1.00	c							
flour, brown	100.00	g	365	7.2	75.5	7.00	427.0	433.0	1.08
						11.20	683.0	693.0	1.73
brown, cooked, no salt, no fat	100.00	g	122	2.7	25.5				
	196.00	g	239	5.4	49.9	5.00	75.00	94.00	1.30
	1.00	c							
wild, cooked	100.00	g	101	4.0	21.3	5.00	20.00	33.00	0.27
	164.00	g	166	6.5	35.0	6.60	26.40	43.60	0.36
	1.00	c							
wild, raw	100.00	g	357	14.7	74.9	0.00	29.00	37.00	0.21
	160.00	g	571	23.6	120.0	0.00	53.90	68.80	0.39
	1.00	c							

OATS

	SERVING QUANTITY	SERVING UNIT	CALORIES (Kcal)	PROTEIN (g)	TOTAL CARBOHYDRATES (g)	SODIUM (mg)	POTASSIUM (mg)	PHOSPHORUS (mg)	TOTAL FAT (g)
raw	100.00	g	379	12.2	67.7	6.00	362.0	410.0	6.52
	81.00	g	307	10.7	54.8	4.86	293.0	332.0	5.28
	1.00	c							
cereal, oat,	100.00	g	372	12.4	73.2	497.00	633.0	357.0	6.60
	33.00	g	123	4.1	24.2	164.00	209.0	118.0	2.18
	1.00	c							
steel cut	100.00	g	378	13.3	66.7	0.00	356.0	na	6.67
Brand:	45.00	g	170	6.0	30.0	0.00	160.0	na	3.00
ARROWHEAD									
MILLS									
	1.00	svg							
rolled	100.00	g	350	12.5	67.5	0.00	350.0	na	6.25
Brand:	40.00	g	140	5.0	27.0	0.00	140.0	na	2.50
MILLVILLE by									
Aldi									
	1.00	svg							
bran, cooked	100.00	g	40	3.2	11.4	1.00	92.00	119.0	0.86
	219.00	g	88	7.0	25.1	2.19	201.0	261.0	1.88
	1.00	c							
bran, uncooked (raw)	100.00	g	246	17.3	66.2	4.00	566.0	734.0	7.03
	94.00	g	231	16.3	62.2	3.76	532.0	690.0	6.61
	1.00	c							
flour, partially debranned	100.00	g	404	14.7	65.7	19.00	371.0	452.0	9.12
	104.00	g	420	15.2	68.3	19.80	386.0	470.0	9.48
	1.00	c							
regular, rolled, not fortified, dry	100.00	g	379	13.2	67.7	6.00	362.0	410.0	6.52
	81.00	g	307	10.7	54.8	4.86	293.0	332.0	5.28
	1.00	c							

WHEAT

	SERVING QUANTITY	SERVING UNIT	CALORIES (kCal)	PROTEIN (g)	TOTAL CARBOHYDRATES (g)	SODIUM (mg)	POTASSIUM (mg)	PHOSPHORUS (mg)	TOTAL FAT (g)
durum	100.00	g	399	13.7	71.1	2.00	431.0	508.0	2.47
	192.00	g	651	26.3	137	3.84	828.0	975.0	4.74
	1.00	c							
sprouted	100.00	g	198	7.5	42.5	16.00	169.0	200.0	1.27
	108.00	g	214	8.1	45.9	17.30	183.0	216.0	1.37
	1.00	c							
germ	100.00	g	360	23.2	51.8	12.00	892.0	842.0	9.72
	115.00	g	414	26.7	59.6	13.80	1,030	968	11.20
	1.00	c							
bran	100.00	g	216	15.6	64.5	2.00	1,180	1,010	4.25
	58.00	g	125	9.1	37.4	1.16	684.0	586.0	2.46
	1.00	c							
cream of wheat, instant, dry	100.00	g	366	10.6	75.5	571.00	115.0	103.0	1.40
	11.50	g	42	1.2	8.7	65.70	13.20	11.80	0.16
	1.00	tbsp							
flour, whole wheat, unenriched	100.00	g	370	15.1	71.2	3.00	376.0	352.0	2.73
whole grain, soft wheat	100.00	g	332	9.6	74.5	3.00	394.0	323.0	1.95
bread flour, unenriched unsifted	100.00	g	361	12.0	72.5	2.00	100.0	97.00	1.66
	137.00	g	495	16.4	99.4	2.74	137.0	133.0	2.27
	1.00	c							
flour, bread, white, enriched	100.00	g	361	12.0	72.5	2.00	100.0	97.00	1.66
	137.00	g	495	16.4	99.4	2.74	137.0	133.0	2.27
	1.00	c							
fllour, cake, enriched unsifted	100.00	g	362	8.2	78.0	2.00	105.0	85.00	0.86
	137.00	g	496	11.2	107.0	2.74	144.0	116.0	1.18
	1.00	c							

CUOSCUOS

	SERVING QUANTITY	SERVING UNIT	CALORIES (kCal)	PROTEIN (g)	TOTAL CARBOHYDRATES (g)	SODIUM (mg)	POTASSIUM (mg)	PHOSPHORUS (mg)	TOTAL FAT (g)
dry	100.00	g	376	12.8	77.4	10.00	166.0	170.0	0.64
	173.00	g	680	22.1	134	17.30	287.0	294.0	1.11
	1.00	c							
cooked	100.00	g	112	3.8	23.2	5.00	58.00	22.00	0.16
	157.00	g	176	6.0	36.4	7.85	91.10	34.50	0.25
	1.00	c							

BARLEY

	SERVING QUANTITY	SERVING UNIT	CALORIES (kCal)	PROTEIN (g)	TOTAL CARBOHYDRATES (g)	SODIUM (mg)	POTASSIUM (mg)	PHOSPHORUS (mg)	TOTAL FAT (g)
pearled, cooked	100.00	g	123	2.3	28.2	3.00	93.00	54.00	0.44
	157.00	g	193	3.6	44.3	4.71	146.0	84.80	0.69
	1.00	c							
flour or meal	100.00	g	345	10.5	74.5	4.00	309.0	296.0	1.60
	148.00	g	511	15.5	110.	5.92	457.0	438.0	2.37
	1.00	c							

QUINOA

	SERVING QUANTITY	SERVING UNIT	CALORIES (kCal)	PROTEIN (g)	TOTAL CARBOHYDRATES (g)	SODIUM (mg)	POTASSIUM (mg)	PHOSPHORUS (mg)	TOTAL FAT (g)
cooked	100.00	g	120	4.4	21.3	7.00	172.0	152.0	1.92
	185.00	g	222	8.1	39.4	13.00	318.0	281.0	3.55
	1.00	c							
uncooked	100.00	g	368	14.1	64.2	5.00	563.0	457.0	6.07
	170.00	g	626	24.0	109	8.50	957.0	777.0	10.30
	1.00	c							
pasta from quinoa flour (gluten-free) not packed	100.00	g	152	3.2	31.1	4.00	63.00	91.00	2.07
	132.00	g	201	4.3	41.1	5.28	83.20	120.0	2.73
	1.00	c							

AMARANTH

	SERVING QUANTITY	SERVING UNIT	CALORIES (kCal)	PROTEIN (g)	TOTAL CARBOHYDRATES (g)	SODIUM (mg)	POTASSIUM (mg)	PHOSPHORUS (mg)	TOTAL FAT (g)
Grain cooked	100.00	g	102	3.8	18.7	6.00	135.0	148.0	1.58
	246.00	g	251	9.4	46.0	14.80	332.0	364.0	3.89
	1.00	c							

CEREALS	SERVING QUANTITY	SERVING UNIT	CALORIES (kcal)	PROTEIN (g)	TOTAL CARBOHYDRATES (g)	SODIUM (mg)	POTASSIUM (mg)	PHOSPHORUS (mg)	TOTAL FAT (g)
corn flakes, plain (store brands)	100.00	g	357	7.5	84.1	729.00	168.0	102.0	0.40
	25.00	g	89	1.9	21.0	182.00	42.00	25.50	0.10
	1.00	c							
corn flakes, frosted (store brands)	100.00	g	389	4.3	90.2	451.00	82.00	46.00	0.87
	40.00	g	156	1.7	36.1	180.00	32.80	18.40	0.35
	1.00	c							
crsipy rice	100.00	g	383	6.7	86.2	545.00	106.0	98.00	1.26
	26.00	g	100	1.7	22.4	142.00	27.60	25.50	0.33
	1.00	c							
cocoa puffs (General Mills)	100.00	g	383	5.6	83.7	564.00	272.0	222.0	5.20
	36.00	g	138	2.0	30.1	203.00	97.90	79.90	1.87
	1.00	c							
muesli, with fruits & nuts	100.00	g	335	8.6	74.9	239.00	324.0	225.0	5.40
	85.00	g	302	7.3	63.7	203.00	275.0	191.0	4.59
	1.00	c							
muesli Brand: Safeway	100.00	g	386	8.8	73.7	228.00	474.0	175.0	5.26
	57.00	g	220	5.0	42.0	130.00	270.0	99.80	3.00
	1.00	svg							
granola, homemade, ready-to-eat	100.00	g	489	13.7	53.9	26.00	539.0	431.0	24.30
	122.00	g	597	16.7	65.8	31.70	658.0	526.0	29.60
	1.00	c							
granola bars, plain	100.00	g	471	10.1	64.4	294.00	336.0	277.0	19.80
	28.00	g	132	2.8	18.0	82.30	94.10	77.60	5.54
	1.00	bar/ oz							
granola bars, almond	100.00	g	495	7.7	62.0	256.00	273.0	228.0	25.50
	28.35	g	140	2.2	17.6	72.60	77.40	64.60	7.23
	1.00	oz							

PANCAKE	SERVING QUANTITY	SERVING UNIT	CALORIES (kCal)	PROTEIN (g)	TOTAL CARBOHYDRATES (g)	SODIUM (mg)	POTASSIUM (mg)	PHOSPHORUS (mg)	TOTAL FAT (g)
buttermilk	100.00	g	227	6.8	28.7	522.00	145.0	139.0	9.30
(from recipe)	38.00	g	86	2.6	10.9	198.00	55.10	52.80	3.53
	1- 4" diameter	pc							
plain,	100.00	g	227	6.4	28.3	439.00	132.0	159.0	9.70
(prepared	38.00	g	86	2.4	10.8	167.00	50.20	60.40	3.69
from recipe)	1- 4" diameter	pc							
plain,	100.00	g	269	5.7	57.3	429.00	97.00	190.0	1.90
reduced fat	105.00	g	282	6.0	60.2	450.00	102.0	200.0	2.00
	3.00	pcs							
plain, frozen, ready to heat	100.00	g	233	5.2	37.8	461.00	90.00	215.0	6.83
includes buttermilk	40.00	g	93	2.1	15.1	184.00	36.00	86.00	2.73
	1 (4")	pc							
gluten-free, frozen, ready	100.00	g	215	3.3	40.3	331.00	127.0	306.0	4.55
to heat	48.00	g	103	1.6	19.3	159.00	61.00	147.0	2.18
	1.00	pc							
WAFFLE									
plain,	100.00	g	291	7.9	32.9	511.00	159.0	190.0	14.10
prepared	75.00	g	218	5.9	24.7	383.00	119.0	142.0	10.60
from recipe	1 (7")	pc							

E. Milk and Cheeses

(Dairy and Non-Dairy)

Hey there!

Do you need to print out this Food List?

You can download a printable version of this chart by scanning the QR code below or copying the link on your computer browser.

https://go.renaltracker.com/printfoodlist

MILK

	SERVING QUANTITY	SERVING UNIT	CALORIES (kcal)	PROTEIN (g)	TOTAL CARBOHYDRATES (g)	SODIUM (mg)	POTASSIUM (mg)	PHOSPHORUS (mg)	TOTAL FAT (g)
(cow) whole	100	g	60	3.3	4.7	38.0	150.0	101.0	3.20
	244	g	146	8.0	11.4	92.7	366.0	246.0	7.81
	1	c							
2% reduced fat	100	g	50	3.4	4.9	39.0	159.0	103.0	1.90
	244	g	122	8.2	12.0	95.2	388.0	251.0	4.64
	1	c							
low fat (1%)	100	g	43	3.4	5.2	39.0	159.0	103.0	0.95
	244	g	105	8.3	12.7	95.2	388.0	251.0	2.32
	1	c							
skim, fat free	100	g	34	3.4	4.9	41.0	167.0	107.0	0.08
	244	g	83	8.4	11.9	100.0	407.0	261.0	0.20
	1	c							
lactose free, from whole milk	100	g	60	3.3	4.7	38.0	150.0	101.0	3.20
	244	g	146	8.0	11.4	92.7	366.0	246.0	7.81
	1	c							
Buttermilk, dried	100	g	387	34.3	49.0	517.0	1592	933	5.78
	6.5	g	25	2.2	3.2	33.6	103.0	60.60	0.38
	1	tbsp							
buttermilk, fluid, whole	100	g	62	3.2	4.9	105.0	135.0	85.00	3.31
	245	g	152	7.9	12.0	257.0	331.0	208.0	8.11
	1	c							
condensed, sweetened	100	g	321	7.9	54.4	127.0	371.0	253.0	8.70
	38	g	122	3.0	20.7	48.3	141.0	96.10	3.31
	1	fl oz							
evaporated, whole	100	g	134	6.8	10.0	106.0	303.0	203.0	7.56
	31.5	g	42	2.1	3.2	33.4	95.40	63.90	2.38
	1	fl oz							
malted	100	g	64	3.2	8.7	60.0	150.0	98.00	1.91
	256	g	164	8.2	22.2	154.0	384.0	251.0	4.89
	1	c							
chocolate	100	g	67	3.4	13.5	79.0	182.0	101.0	0.00
	248	g	166	8.4	33.4	196.0	451.0	250.0	0.00
	1	c							
strawberry (whole milk)	100	g	85	3.0	11.8	38.0	139.0	94.00	2.97
	248	g	211	7.5	29.3	94.2	345.0	233.0	7.37
	1	c							

MILK

MILK	SERVING QUANTITY	SERVING UNIT	CALORIES (kCal)	PROTEIN (g)	TOTAL CARBOHYDRATES (g)	SODIUM (mg)	POTASSIUM (mg)	PHOSPHORUS (mg)	TOTAL FAT (g)
SOY	100	g	43	2.6	4.9	47.0	122.0	43.00	1.47
	244	g	105	6.3	12.0	115.0	298.0	105.0	3.59
	1	c							
soy, light	100	g	30	2.4	3.5	48.0	117.0	87.00	0.77
	244	g	73	5.8	8.6	117.0	285.0	212.0	1.88
	1	c							
soy, chocolate	100	g	63	2.3	10.0	53.0	143.0	51.00	1.53
	244	g	154	5.5	24.3	129.0	349.0	124.0	3.73
	1	c							
soy, non-fat	100	g	28	2.5	4.1	57.0	105.0	87.00	0.04
	244	g	68	6.0	10.1	139.0	256.0	212.0	0.10
	1	c							
RICE	100	g	47	0.3	9.2	39.0	27.00	56.00	0.97
	244	g	115	0.7	22.4	95.2	65.90	137.0	2.37
	1	c							
rice milk, unsweetened	100	g	47	0.3	9.2	39.0	27.00	56.00	0.97
	240	g	113	0.7	22.0	93.6	64.80	134.0	2.33
	8	fl oz							
ALMOND, unsweeteened	100	g	15	0.4	1.3	72.0	67.00	9.00	0.96
	244	g	37	1.0	3.2	176.0	163.0	22.00	2.34
	1	c							
almond, unsweeteened, chocolate	100	g	16	0.5	1.5	72.0	71.00	11.00	1.00
	244	g	39	1.1	3.6	176.0	173.0	26.80	2.44
	1	c							
almond milk, sweeteend	100	g	30	0.4	5.2	69.0	64.00	9.00	0.93
	244	g	73	0.9	12.8	168.0	156.0	22.00	2.27
	1	c							
almond, sweetened, chocolate	100	g	41	0.4	8.3	67.0	67.00	11.00	0.95
	244	g	100	1.1	20.4	163.0	163.0	26.80	2.32
	1	c							
COCONUT	100	g	31	0.2	2.9	19.0	19.00	0.00	2.08
	244	g	76	0.5	7.1	46.4	46.40	0.00	5.08
	1	c							
GOAT, whole	100	g	69	3.6	4.5	50.0	204.0	111.0	4.14
	244	g	168	8.7	10.9	122.0	498.0	271.0	10.10
	1	c							

MILK
SUBSTITUTE

	SERVING QUANTITY	SERVING UNIT	CALORIES (kCal)	PROTEIN (g)	TOTAL CARBOHYDRATES (g)	SODIUM (mg)	POTASSIUM (mg)	PHOSPHORUS (mg)	TOTAL FAT (g)
Non-dairy milk/creamer	100	g	29	1.0	3.8	60.0	80.00	19.00	1.17
	30.5	g	9	0.3	1.1	18.3	24.40	5.80	0.36
	1	fl oz							
imitation, non-soy	100	g	46	1.6	5.3	55.0	150.0	100.0	2.00
	244	g	112	3.9	12.9	134.0	366.0	244.0	4.88
	1	cup							
Kefir	100	g	52	3.6	7.5	38.0	159.0	100.0	0.96
	244	g	127	8.8	18.3	92.7	388.0	244	2.34
	1	c							
Sorbet	100	g	110	0.8	27.1	13.0	28.00	3.00	0.05
	80	g	88	0.6	21.7	10.4	22.40	2.40	0.04
	1	bar							

YOGURT

	SERVING QUANTITY	SERVING UNIT	CALORIES (kCal)	PROTEIN (g)	TOTAL CARBOHYDRATES (g)	SODIUM (mg)	POTASSIUM (mg)	PHOSPHORUS (mg)	TOTAL FAT (g)
coconut milk, yogurt	100	g	64	0.3	8.0	21.0	27.00	2.00	3.50
	170	g	109	0.5	13.5	35.7	45.90	3.40	5.95
	6	oz							
dressing	100	g	220	3.5	11.8	43.0	146.0	85.00	18.27
	15.4	g	34	0.5	1.8	6.6	22.50	13.10	2.81
	1	tbsp							
liquid	100	g	72	3.7	11.8	53.0	171.0	103.0	1.09
	245	g	176	9.1	28.9	130.0	419.0	252.0	2.67
	1	c							
plain, whole milk	100	g	61	3.5	4.7	46.0	155.0	95.00	3.25
	227	g	138	7.9	10.6	104.0	352.0	216.0	7.38
	8	oz							
	100	g	87	3.1	12.4	44.0	146.0	86.00	2.87
Whole milk with fruit	170	g	148	5.3	21.0	74.8	248.0	146.0	4.88
	6	oz							

YOGURT

	SERVING QUANTITY	SERVING UNIT	CALORIES (kcal)	PROTEIN (g)	TOTAL CARBOHYDRATES (g)	SODIUM (mg)	POTASSIUM (mg)	PHOSPHORUS (mg)	TOTAL FAT (g)
whole milk, flavored (non-fruit)	100	g	77	3.3	9.4	44.0	147.0	90.00	3.10
	170	g	131	5.6	16.0	74.8	250.0	153.0	5.27
	6	oz							
non-fat milk, plain, vanilla	100	g	78	2.9	17.0	47.0	141.0	88.00	0.00
	227	g	177	6.7	38.7	107.0	320.0	200.0	0.00
	8	oz							
non-fat milk, fruit	100	g	83	5.1	15.0	72.0	234.0	140.0	0.17
	170	g	141	8.7	25.5	122.0	398.0	238.0	0.29
	6	oz							
Soy, yogurt, plain	100	g	94	3.5	16.0	35.0	47.00	38.00	1.80
	170	g	160	6.0	27.1	59.5	79.90	64.60	3.06
	6	oz							
Greek, plain, whole milk	100	g	97	9.0	4.0	35.0	141.0	135.0	5.00
	170	g	165	15.3	6.8	59.5	240.0	230.0	8.50
	6	oz							
Greek, fruit, whole milk	100	g	106	7.3	12.3	37.0	113.0	109.0	3.00
	170	g	180	12.5	20.9	62.9	192.0	185.0	5.10
	6	oz							
Greek, flavored, other than fruit	100	g	111	8.5	9.4	39.0	121.0	117.0	4.44
	170	g	189	14.4	15.9	66.3	206.0	199.0	7.55
	6	oz							
Greek, plain, low fat	100	g	73	10.0	3.9	34.0	141.0	137.0	1.92
	170	g	124	16.9	6.7	57.8	240.0	233.0	3.26
	6	oz							
Greek, LF, flavors other than fruit	100	g	95	8.6	9.5	40.0	123.0	119.0	2.50
	170	g	162	14.7	16.2	68.0	209.0	202.0	4.25
	6	oz							
Greek, non-fat (NF), plain	100	g	59	10.2	3.6	36.0	141.0	135.0	0.39
	170	g	100	17.3	6.1	61.2	240.0	230.0	0.66
	6	oz							
Greek, NF, flavors other than fruit	100	g	78	8.6	10.4	34.0	123.0	119.0	0.18
	170	g	133	14.7	17.6	57.8	209.0	202.0	0.31
	6	oz							
Frozen yogurt, chocolate	100	g	131	3.0	21.6	63.0	234.0	89.00	3.60
	160	g	210	4.8	34.6	101.0	374.0	142.0	5.76
1 scoop= small cup	1	scoop							

YOGURT

	SERVING QUANTITY	SERVING UNIT	CALORIES (kCal)	PROTEIN (g)	TOTAL CARBOHYDRATES (g)	SODIUM (mg)	POTASSIUM (mg)	PHOSPHORUS (mg)	TOTAL FAT (g)
Frozen yogurt, vanilla	100	g	127	3.0	21.6	63.0	156.0	89.00	3.60
	160	g	203	4.8	34.6	101.0	250.0	142.0	5.76
1 scoop= small cup	1	scoop							
Frozen yogurt, soft serve, chocolate	100	g	160	4.3	24.9	86.0	237.0	141.0	5.76
	175	g	280	7.5	43.5	150.0	415.0	247.0	10.10
	1	c							
Frozn yogurt, soft serve, vanilla	100	g	159	4.0	24.2	87.0	211.0	129.0	5.60
	175	g	278	7.0	42.4	152.0	369.0	226.0	9.80
	1	c							
Frozn yogurt bar, vanilla	100	g	127	3.0	21.6	63.0	156.0	89.00	3.60
	65	g	83	2.0	14.0	41.0	101.0	57.80	2.34
	1	bar							
Frozn yogurt bar, chocolate	100	g	131	3.0	21.6	63.0	234.0	89.00	3.60
	65	g	85	2.0	14.0	41.0	152.0	57.80	2.34
	1	bar							
Frozn yogurt cone, vanilla	100	g	139	3.2	23.9	71.0	154.0	89.00	3.73
	125	g	174	4.0	29.9	88.8	192.0	111.0	4.66
	1	cone							
Frozn yogurt cone, chocolate	100	g	142	3.2	23.9	71.0	229.0	89.00	3.73
	125	g	178	4.0	29.9	88.8	286.0	111.0	4.66
	1	cone							
Frozn yogurt, waffle cone, vanilla	100	g	143	3.3	25.3	77.0	155.0	90.00	3.61
	255	g	365	8.4	64.5	196.0	395.0	230.0	9.20
	1	cone							
Frozn yogurt, waffle cone, choco	100	g	147	3.3	25.3	77.0	229.0	90.00	3.61
	255	g	375	8.4	64.5	196.0	584.0	230.0	9.20
	1	cone							

CHEESE	SERVING QUANTITY	SERVING UNIT	CALORIES (kcal)	PROTEIN (g)	TOTAL CARBOHYDRATES (g)	SODIUM (mg)	POTASSIUM (mg)	PHOSPHORUS (mg)	TOTAL FAT (g)
mozzarella, from whole milk	100	g	299	22.2	2.4	486.0	76.00	354.0	22.14
shredded	112	g	335	24.8	2.7	544.0	85.10	396.0	24.80
	1	c							
mozzarella, part skim milk	100	g	254	24.3	2.8	619.0	84.00	463.0	15.92
	28.35	g	72	6.9	0.8	175.0	23.80	131.0	4.51
	1	oz							
Mozzarella, reduced sodium (shredded)	100	g	280	27.5	3.1	16.0	95.00	524.0	17.10
	113	g	316	31.1	3.5	18.1	107.0	592.0	19.30
	1	cup							
ricotta, from whole milk	100	g	158	7.8	6.9	105.0	230.0	162.0	11.00
	129	g	204	10.1	8.9	135.0	297.0	209.0	14.20
	0.5	c							
riccota, part skim milk	100	g	138	11.4	5.1	99.0	125.0	183.0	7.91
	124	g	171	14.1	6.4	123.0	155.0	227.0	9.81
	0.5	c							
cream cheese, regular	100	g	295	7.1	3.5	436.0	112.0	91.00	28.60
	28.35	g	84	2.0	1.0	124.0	31.80	25.80	8.11
	1	oz							
cream cheese, light	100	g	201	7.9	8.1	359.0	247.0	152.0	15.28
	28.35	g	57	2.2	2.3	102.0	70.00	43.10	4.33
	1	oz							
processed cheese food	100	g	307	16.1	8.9	1279.0	295.0	768.0	23.06
	21	g	65	3.4	1.9	269.0	62.00	161.0	4.84
	1	slice							
Cottage cheese	100	g	84	11.0	4.3	321.0	120.0	148.0	2.30
	210	g	176	23.1	9.1	674.0	252.0	311.0	4.83
	1	cup							
cottage cheese. low fat	100	g	84	11.0	4.3	321.0	120.0	148.0	2.30
	226	g	190	24.9	9.7	725.0	271.0	334.0	5.20
	1	cup							
Monterey shredded	100	g	373	24.5	0.7	600.0	81.00	444.0	30.28
	113	g	421	27.7	0.8	678.0	91.50	502.0	34.20
	1	cup							
Cheddar	100	g	408	23.3	2.4	654.0	77.00	458.0	34.00
	21	g	86	4.9	0.5	137.0	16.20	96.20	7.14
	1	slice							

CHEESE

	SERVING QUANTITY	SERVING UNIT	CALORIES (kCal)	PROTEIN (g)	TOTAL CARBOHYDRATES (g)	SODIUM (mg)	POTASSIUM (mg)	PHOSPHORUS (mg)	TOTAL FAT (g)
Cheddar, reduced sodium	100	g	398	24.4	1.9	21.0	112.00	484.0	32.62
	21	g	84	5.1	0.4	4.4	23.50	102.0	6.85
	1	slice							
Cheddar, sharp sliced	100	g	410	24.3	2.1	644.0	76.00	460.0	33.82
	28	g	115	6.8	0.6	180.0	21.30	129.0	9.47
	1	oz							
Cheddar/ American cheese spread	100	g	290	16.4	8.7	1625	242.00	875.0	21.23
	21	g	61	3.5	1.8	341.0	50.80	184.0	4.46
	1	wedge							
American	100	g	307	16.1	8.9	1279.	295.00	768.0	23.06
	21	g	65	3.4	1.9	269.0	62.00	161.0	4.84
	1	slice							
Brick	100	g	371	23.2	2.8	560.0	136.00	451.0	29.68
	17.2	g	64	4.0	0.5	96.3	23.40	77.60	5.10
	1	cubic inch							
Brie	100	g	334	20.8	0.5	629.0	152.00	188.0	27.68
	17	g	57	3.5	0.1	107.0	25.80	32.00	4.71
	1	cubic inch							
blue	100	g	353	21.4	2.3	1146	256.00	387.0	28.74
	28.35	g	100	6.1	0.7	325.0	72.60	110.0	8.15
	1	oz							
Camembert	100	g	300	19.8	0.5	842.0	187.00	347.0	24.26
	38	g	114	7.5	0.2	320.0	71.10	132.0	9.22
1 wedge = 1.33 oz	1	wedge							
Colby	100	g	394	23.8	2.6	604.0	127.00	457.0	32.11
	21	g	83	5.0	0.5	127.0	26.70	96.00	6.74
	1	slice							
Caraway	100	g	376	25.2	1.1	690.0	93.00	490.0	29.20
	28.35	g	107	7.1	0.9	196.0	26.40	139.0	8.28
	1	oz							
Edam	100	g	356	24.9	2.2	819.0	121.00	546.0	27.44
	21	g	75	5.2	0.5	172.0	25.40	115.0	5.76
	1	slice							
Feta	100	g	265	14.2	3.9	1139.	62.00	337.0	21.49
	17	g	45	2.4	0.7	194.0	10.50	57.30	3.62
	1	cubic inch							
Fontina	100	g	389	25.6	1.6	800.0	64.00	346.0	31.14
	21	g	82	5.4	0.3	168.0	13.40	72.70	6.54
	1	slice							
goat	100	g	364	21.6	0.1	415.0	158.00	375.0	29.84
	25	g	91	5.4	0.0	104.0	39.50	93.80	7.46
	1	cubic inch							

CHEESE	SERVING QUANTITY	SERVING UNIT	CALORIES (kCal)	PROTEIN (g)	TOTAL CARBOHYDRATES (g)	SODIUM (mg)	POTASSIUM (mg)	PHOSPHORUS (mg)	TOTAL FAT (g)
Gouda	100	g	356	24.9	2.2	819.0	121.0	546.0	27.44
	28.35	g	101	7.0	0.6	232.0	34.30	155.0	7.78
	1	oz							
Gruyere	100	g	413	29.8	0.4	714.0	81.00	605.0	32.34
	21	g	87	6.3	0.1	150.0	17.00	127.0	6.70
	1	slice							
Blue or Roquefort	100	g	353	21.4	2.3	1146.0	256.0	387.0	28.74
	17.3	g	61	3.7	0.4	198.0	44.30	67.00	4.97
	1	cubic inch							
Colby Jack	100	g	384	24.1	1.6	602.0	104.0	450.0	31.20
	21	g	81	5.1	0.3	126.0	21.80	94.50	6.55
	1	slice							
Parmesan, grated	100	g	420	29.6	12.4	1750.0	184.0	634.0	28.00
	7.6	g	32	2.3	0.9	133.0	14.00	48.20	1.82
	1	tbsp							
Parmesan, hard	100	g	421	29.6	12.4	1750.0	184.0	634.0	28.00
	10.3	g	43	3.1	1.3	180.0	19.00	65.30	2.88
	1	cubic inch							
Mexican blend shredded	100	g	358	23.5	1.8	607.0	85.00	438.0	28.51
	113	g	405	26.6	2.0	686.0	96.00	495.0	32.20
	1	cup							
Mexican blend, reduced fat shredded	100	g	282	24.7	3.4	776.0	93.00	583.0	19.40
	113	g	319	27.9	3.9	877.0	105.0	659.0	21.90
	1	cup							
Muenster	100	g	368	23.4	1.1	628.0	134.0	468.0	30.04
	21	g	77	5.0	0.2	132.0	28.10	98.30	6.31
	1	slice							
Neufchatel	100	g	253	9.2	3.6	334.0	152.0	138.0	22.78
	28.35	g	72	2.6	1.0	94.7	43.10	39.10	6.46
	1	oz							
Provolone	100	g	351	25.6	2.1	727.0	138.0	496.0	26.62
	21	g	74	5.4	0.4	153.0	29.00	104.0	5.59
	1	slice							
Romano	100	g	387	31.8	3.6	1433.0	86.00	760.0	26.94
	28.35	g	110	9.0	1.0	406.0	24.40	215.0	7.64
	1	oz							
Swiss	100	g	393	27.0	1.4	185.0	71.00	574.0	31.00
	21	g	83	5.7	0.3	38.8	14.90	121.0	6.51
	1	slice							
Tilsiter/ Tilsit	100	g	340	24.4	1.9	753.0	65.00	500.0	25.98
	28.35	g	96	6.9	0.5	213.0	18.40	142.0	7.36
	1	oz							

CREAM

	SERVING QUANTITY	SERVING UNIT	CALORIES (kCal)	PROTEIN (g)	TOTAL CARBOHYDRATES (g)	SODIUM (mg)	POTASSIUM (mg)	PHOSPHORUS (mg)	TOTAL FAT (g)
sour cream, regular	100	g	198	2.4	4.6	31.0	125.00	76.00	19.35
	30	g	59	0.7	1.4	9.3	37.50	22.80	5.80
	1	container							
sour cream, light	100	g	136	3.5	7.1	83.0	212.00	71.00	10.60
	240	g	326	8.4	17.0	199.0	509.00	170.0	25.40
	1	cup							
sour cream, imitation	100	g	208	2.4	6.6	102.0	161.00	45.00	19.52
	240	g	499	5.8	15.9	245.0	386.00	108.0	46.80
	1	cup							
sour cream, fat free	100	g	74	3.1	15.6	141.0	129.00	95.00	0.00
	240	g	178	7.4	37.4	338.0	310.00	228.0	0.00
	1	cup							
heavy full cream	100	g	340	2.8	2.8	27.0	95.00	58.00	36.08
	30	g	102	0.9	1.0	8.1	28.50	17.40	10.80
	1	fl oz							
whipped	100	g	343	2.7	8.6	26.0	89.00	55.00	33.94
	40	g	137	1.1	3.4	10.4	35.60	22.00	13.60
	1	cup							
half and half	100	g	131	3.1	4.3	61.0	132.00	95.00	11.50
	30	g	39	0.9	1.3	18.3	39.60	28.50	3.45
	1	fl oz							
coffee, light cream	100	g	195	3.0	3.7	72.0	136.00	92.00	19.10
	11	g	21	0.3	0.4	7.9	15.00	10.10	2.10
	1	ind. container							

F. Fats

(Oils, Nuts, & Seeds)

Hey there!

Do you need to print out this Food List?

You can download a printable version of this chart by scanning the QR code below or copying the link on your computer browser.

ALMOND

	SERVING QUANTITY	SERVING UNIT	CALORIES (kCal)	PROTEIN (g)	TOTAL CARBOHYDRATES (g)	SODIUM (mg)	POTASSIUM (mg)	PHOSPHORUS (mg)	TOTAL FAT (g)
whole	100	g	579	21.2	21.6	1.00	733.00	481.00	49.9
	35.75	g	207	7.6	7.7	0.36	262.05	171.96	17.9
	0.25	c							
slivered	100	g	579	21.2	21.6	1.00	733.00	481.00	49.9
	27	g	156	5.7	5.8	0.27	197.91	129.87	13.5
	0.25	c							
ground	100	g	579	21.2	21.6	1.00	733.00	481.00	49.9
	23.75	g	138	5.0	5.1	0.24	174.09	114.42	11.9
	0.25	c							
paste (marzipan)	100	g	458	9.0	47.8	9.00	314.00	258.00	27.7
	28.38	g	130	2.6	13.6	2.55	89.10	73.21	7.9
	2	tbsp							
oil	100	g	884	0.0	0.0	0.00	0.00	0.00	100.0
	13.6	g	120	0.0	0.0	0.00	0.00	0.00	13.6
	1	tbsp							
butter, without salt added	100	g	614	21.0	18.8	227.0	748.00	508.00	55.5
	16	g	98	3.4	3.0	1.12	119.68	81.28	8.9
	1	tbsp							
dry roasted, without salt added	100	g	598	3.0	21.0	3.00	713.00	471.00	52.5
	34.5	g	206	7.2	7.3	1.04	245.99	162.50	18.1
	0.25	c							
oil roasted, without salt	100	g	607	21.2	17.7	1.00	699.00	466.00	55.2
	39.25	g	238	8.3	6.9	0.39	274.36	182.91	21.7
	0.25	c							
milk, unsweetened, shelf stable	100	g	15	0.4	1.3	72.00	67.00	9.00	1.0
	262	g	39	1.1	3.4	188.6	175.54	23.58	2.5
	1	c							
milk, sweetened, vanilla flavor ready-to-drink	100	g	38	0.4	6.6	63.00	50.00	8.00	1.0
	240	g	91	1.0	15.8	151.2	120.00	19.20	2.5
	1	c							
milk, chocolate flavor, unsweetened fortified Vit. D2 and E	100	g	21	0.8	1.3	75.00	96.00	17.00	1.5
	240	g	50	2.0	3.0	180.0	130.40	40.80	3.5
	1	c							

WALNUT	SERVING QUANTITY	SERVING UNIT	CALORIES (kCal)	PROTEIN (g)	TOTAL CARBOHYDRATES (g)	SODIUM (mg)	POTASSIUM (mg)	PHOSPHORUS (mg)	TOTAL FAT (g)
english, halves	100	g	654	15.2	13.7	2.00	441.00	346.0	65.2
	25	g	164	3.8	3.4	0.50	110.25	86.50	16.3
	0.25	c							
english, ground	100	g	654	15.2	13.7	2.00	441.00	346.0	65.2
	20	g	131	3.1	2.7	0.40	88.20	69.20	13.0
	0.25	c							
english, chopped	100	g	654	15.2	13.7	2.00	441.00	346.0	65.2
	29.25	g	191	4.5	4.0	0.59	128.99	101.2	19.1
	0.25	c							
butternut or white walnut, dried	100	g	612	24.9	12.1	1.00	421.00	446.0	57.0
	120	g	734	29.9	14.5	1.20	505.20	535.2	68.4
	1	c							
black or american, dried, chopped	100	g	619	24.1	9.6	2.00	523.00	513.0	59.3
	31.25	g	193	7.5	3.0	0.63	163.44	160.3	18.5
	0.25	c							
black or american, dried, ground	100	g	604	23.5	9.3	1.95	509.92	500.2	57.9
	26.67	g	161	6.3	2.5	0.52	135.98	133.4	15.4
	0.33	c							
glazed	100	g	500	8.3	47.6	446.0	232.00	na	35.7
	28.35	g	142	2.4	13.5	126.5	65.77	na	10.1
	1	oz							
oil	100	g	884	0.0	0.0	0.0	0.00	0.00	100.0
	13.6	g	120	0.0	0.0	0.0	0.00	0.00	13.6
	1	tbsp							

	SERVING QUANTITY	SERVING UNIT	CALORIES (kCal)	PROTEIN (g)	TOTAL CARBOHYDRATES (g)	SODIUM (mg)	POTASSIUM (mg)	PHOSPHORUS (mg)	TOTAL FAT (g)
PECANS									
chopped	100	g	691	9.2	13.9	0.00	410.00	277.00	72.0
	109	g	753	10.0	15.1	0.00	446.90	410.00	78.5
	1	c							
halves	100	g	691	9.2	13.9	0.00	410.00	277.00	72.0
	24.75	g	171	2.3	3.4	0.00	101.48	68.56	17.8
	0.25	c							
halves, oil roasted	100	g	715	9.2	13.0	1.00	392.00	263.00	75.2
	110	g	787	10.1	14.3	1.10	431.20	289.30	82.8
	1	c							
dry roasted, without salt added	100	g	710	9.5	13.6	1.00	424.00	293.00	74.3
	28.35	g	201	2.7	3.8	0.28	120.20	83.07	21.1
	1	oz							
PISTACHIO									
raw	100	g	560	20.2	27.2	1.00	1,025	490.00	45.3
(1 oz = 49 kernels)	123	g	689	24.8	33.4	1.23	1,261	602.70	55.7
	1	c							
dry roasted, no salt added	100	g	572	21.1	28.3	6.00	1,007	469.00	45.8
	123	g	704	25.9	34.8	7.38	1,239	576.87	56.4
	1	c							
MACADAMIA									
whole or halves	100	g	718	7.9	13.8	5.00	368.00	188.00	75.8
(1 oz = 10-12 kernels)	134	g	962	10.6	18.5	6.70	493.12	251.92	101.5
	1	c							
dry roasted, without salt added	100	g	718	7.8	13.4	4.00	363.00	198.00	76.1
	33.5	g	241	2.6	4.5	1.34	121.61	66.33	25.5
	0.25	c							

81

CASHEW	SERVING QUANTITY	SERVING UNIT	CALORIES (kCal)	PROTEIN (g)	TOTAL CARBOHYDRATES (g)	SODIUM (mg)	POTASSIUM (mg)	PHOSPHORUS (mg)	TOTAL FAT (g)
raw	100	g	553	18.2	30.2	12.00	660.00	593.0	43.9
	28.35	g	157	5.2	8.6	3.40	187.11	168.1	12.4
	1	oz							
oil roasted, no salt added	100	g	580	16.8	29.9	13.00	632.00	531.0	47.8
	129	g	748	21.7	38.5	16.77	815.28	685	61.6
	1	c							
dry roasted, no salt aded (halves and whole)	100	g	574	15.3	32.7	16.00	565.00	490.0	46.4
	137	g	786	21.0	44.8	21.92	774.05	671.3	63.5
	1	c							
butter, without salt added	100	g	587	17.6	27.6	15.00	546.00	457.0	49.4
	32	g	188	5.6	8.8	4.80	174.72	146.3	15.8
	2	tbsp							
HAZELNUT									
oil	100	g	884	0.0	0.0	0.00	0.00	0.00	100.0
	13.6	g	120	0.0	0.0	0.00	0.00	0.00	13.6
	1	tbsp							
whole (1 oz= 21 kernels)	100	g	628	15.0	16.7	0.00	680.00	290.0	60.8
	33.75	g	212	5.1	5.6	0.00	229.50	97.88	20.5
	0.25	c							
blanched	100	g	629	13.7	17.0	0.00	658.00	310.0	61.2
	28.35	g	178	3.9	4.8	0.00	186.54	87.89	17.3
	1	oz							
chopped	100	g	628	15.0	16.7	0.00	680.00	290.0	60.8
	28.75	g	181	4.3	4.8	0.00	195.50	83.38	17.5
	0.25	c							
ground	100	g	628	15.0	16.7	0.00	680.00	290.0	60.8
	18.75	g	118	2.8	3.1	0.00	127.50	54.38	11.4
	0.25	c							
dry roasted, without salt added	100	g	646	15.0	17.6	0.00	755.00	310.0	62.4
	28.35	g	183	4.3	5.0	0.00	214.04	87.89	17.7
	1	oz							
spread, chocolate flavored	100	g	539	5.4	62.4	41.00	407.00	152.0	29.7

PEANUT	SERVING QUANTITY	SERVING UNIT	CALORIES (kCal)	PROTEIN (g)	TOTAL CARBOHYDRATES (g)	SODIUM (mg)	POTASSIUM (mg)	PHOSPHORUS (mg)	TOTAL FAT (g)
oil	100	g	884	0.0	0.0	0.00	0.00	0.00	100.0
	13.5	g	119	0.0	0.0	0.00	0.00	0.00	13.5
	1	tbsp							
all types	100	g	567	25.8	16.1	18.00	705.00	376.00	49.2
	36.5	g	207	9.4	5.9	6.57	257.33	137.24	18.0
	0.25	c							
all types, dry roasted, no salt added (1 0z = 28.35g)	100	g	587	24.4	21.4	6.00	634.00	363.00	49.7
	36.5	g	214	8.9	7.8	2.19	231.41	132.50	18.1
	0.25	c							
all types, oil roasted, no salt	100	g	599	28.0	15.3	6.00	726.00	397.00	52.5
	133	g	797	37.3	20.3	7.98	965.58	528.01	69.8
	1	c							
butter, smooth, reduced fat	100	g	520	25.9	36.7	540.0	669.00	369.00	34.0
	36	g	187	9.3	12.8	194.4	240.84	132.84	12.2
	2	tbsp							
butter, smooth, no salt added	100	g	598	22.2	22.3	17.00	558.00	335.00	51.4
	32	g	191	7.1	7.1	5.44	178.56	107.20	16.4
	2	tbsp							
butter, chunky, no salt added	100	g	589	24.1	21.6	17.00	745.00	319.00	49.9
	32	g	188	7.7	6.9	5.44	238.40	102.08	16.0
	2	tbsp							
butter, reduced sodium	100	g	590	24.0	21.8	203.0	747.00	317.00	49.9
	16	g	94	3.8	3.5	32.48	119.52	50.72	8.0
	1	tbsp							
sauce, made with PB, water & soy sauce	100	g	257	6.3	22.0	1338	235.00	107.00	16.0
	18	g	46	1.1	4.0	240.8	42.30	19.26	2.9
	1	tbsp							
brittle	100	g	486	7.6	71.2	445.0	168.00	106.00	19.0
	42.53	g	207	3.2	30.3	189.2	71.44	45.08	8.1
	1.5	oz							
flour, defatted	100	g	327	52.2	34.7	180.0	1,290	760.00	0.6
	30	g	98	15.7	10.4	54.00	387.00	228.00	0.2
	0.5	c							

	SERVING QUANTITY	SERVING UNIT	CALORIES (kCal)	PROTEIN (g)	TOTAL CARBOHYDRATES (g)	SODIUM (mg)	POTASSIUM (mg)	PHOSPHORUS (mg)	TOTAL FAT (g)
PINE									
(Pinyon), dried	100	g	629	11.6	19.3	72.00	628.00	35.00	61.0
	28.35	g	178	3.3	5.5	20.41	178.04	9.92	17.3
	1	oz							
(Pignolia), dried	100	g	673	13.7	13.1	2.00	597.00	575.0	68.4
	8.6	g	58	1.2	1.1	0.17	51.34	49.45	5.9
	1	tbsp							
CHESTNUT									
Japanese	100	g	154	2.3	34.9	14.00	329.00	72.00	0.5
	28.35	g	44	0.6	9.9	3.97	93.27	20.41	0.2
	1	oz							
Chinese	100	g	224	4.2	49.1	3.00	447.00	96.00	1.1
	28.35	g	64	1.2	13.9	0.85	126.72	27.22	0.3
	1	oz							
European, unpeeled	100	g	213	2.4	45.5	3.00	518.00	93.00	2.3
	36.25	g	77	0.9	16.5	1.09	187.78	33.71	0.8
	0.25	c							
European, peeled	100	g	196	1.6	44.2	2.00	484.00	38.00	1.3
	28.35	g	56	0.5	12.5	0.57	137.21	10.77	0.4
	1	oz							
European, roasted	100	g	245	3.2	53.0	2.00	592.00	107.0	2.2
	28.35	g	69	0.9	15.0	0.57	167.83	30.33	0.6
	1	oz							
Japanese, roasted	100	g	201	3.0	45.1	19.00	427.00	93.00	0.8
	28.35	g	57	0.8	12.8	5.39	121.05	26.37	0.2
	1	oz							
Chinese, roasted	100	g	239	4.5	52.4	4.00	477.00	102.0	1.2
	28.35	g	68	1.3	14.8	1.13	135.23	28.92	0.3
	1	oz							
Chinese, boiled and steamed	100	g	153	2.9	33.6	2.00	306.00	66.00	0.8
	28.35	g	43	0.8	9.5	0.57	86.75	18.71	0.2
	1	oz							
European, boiled and steamed	100	g	131	2.0	27.8	27.00	715.00	99.00	1.4
	28.35	g	37	0.6	7.9	7.65	202.70	15.31	0.4
	1	oz							
Japanese, boiled and steamed	100	g	56	0.8	12.6	5.00	119.00	26.00	0.2
	28.35	g	16	0.2	3.6	1.42	33.74	7.37	0.1
	1	oz							

84

	SERVING QUANTITY	SERVING UNIT	CALORIES (kCal)	PROTEIN (g)	TOTAL CARBOHYDRATES (g)	SODIUM (mg)	POTASSIUM (mg)	PHOSPHORUS (mg)	TOTAL FAT (g)
ACORN									
Nuts	100	g	387	6.2	40.8	0.00	539.00	79.00	23.9
	28.35	g	110	1.7	11.6	0.00	152.81	22.40	6.8
	1	oz							
flour	100	g	501	7.5	54.7	0.00	712.00	103.0	30.2
	28.35	g	142	2.1	15.5	0.00	201.85	29.20	8.6
	1	oz							
nuts, dried	100	g	509	8.1	53.7	0.00	709.00	103.0	31.4
	28.35	g	144	2.3	15.2	0.00	201.00	29.20	8.9
	1	oz							
CHIA									
seeds, dried	100	g	486	16.5	42.1	16.00	407.00	860.0	30.7
	28.35	g	138	4.7	11.9	4.54	115.38	243.8	8.7
	1	oz							
HEMP									
seeds, hulled	100	g	553	31.6	8.7	5.00	1,200	1,650	48.8
	30	g	166	9.5	2.6	1.50	360.00	495.0	14.6
	3	tbsp							
FLAXSEED									
seeds, whole	100	g	534	18.3	28.9	30.00	813.00	642.0	42.2
	10.3	g	55	1.9	3.0	3.09	83.70	66.10	4.3
	1	tbsp							
seeds, ground	7	g	37	1.3	2.0	2.10	56.90	44.90	3.0
	1	tbsp							
oil	100	g	884	0.1	0.0	0.00	0.00	1.00	100.0
	14	g	124	0.0	0.0	0.00	0.00	0.14	14.0
	1	tbsp							
oil with added sliced flaxseed	100	g	878	0.4	0.4	6.00	31.00	27.00	99.0
	13.7	g	120	0.1	0.1	0.82	4.25	3.70	13.6
	1	tbsp							
oil, cold pressed	100	g	884	0.1	0.0	0.00	0.00	1.00	100.0
	13.6	g	120	0.0	0.0	0.00	0.00	0.14	13.6
	1	tbsp							

SESAME

	SERVING QUANTITY	SERVING UNIT	CALORIES (kcal)	PROTEIN (g)	TOTAL CARBOHYDRATES (g)	SODIUM (mg)	POTASSIUM (mg)	PHOSPHORUS (mg)	TOTAL FAT (g)
seeds, kernels, toasted	100	g	567	17.0	26.0	39.00	406.00	774.00	48.0
	128	g	726	21.7	33.3	49.92	519.68	990.72	61.4
	1	c							
butter or Tahini	100	g	592	17.4	21.5	35.00	459.00	790.00	53.0
	30	g	178	5.2	6.5	10.50	137.70	237.00	15.9
	2	tbsp							
seeds, whole, dried	100	g	573	17.7	23.5	11.00	468.00	629.00	49.7
	9	g	52	1.6	2.1	0.99	42.12	56.61	4.5
	1	tbsp							
butter or Tahini, from roasted/toasted kernels	100	g	595	17.0	21.2	115.00	414.00	732.00	53.8
	30	g	179	5.1	6.4	34.50	124.20	219.60	16.1
	2	tbsp							

SUNFLOWER

	SERVING QUANTITY	SERVING UNIT	CALORIES (kcal)	PROTEIN (g)	TOTAL CARBOHYDRATES (g)	SODIUM (mg)	POTASSIUM (mg)	PHOSPHORUS (mg)	TOTAL FAT (g)
seeds, kernels, toasted	100	g	619	17.2	20.6	3.00	491.00	1,158	56.8
	33.5	g	207	5.8	6.9	1.01	164.49	387.93	19.0
	0.25	c							
seeds, kernels, dried	100	g	584	20.8	20.0	9.00	645.00	660.00	51.5
	36	g	210	7.5	7.2	3.24	232.20	237.60	18.5
	0.25	c							
seeds, kernels, oil roasted	100	g	592	20.1	22.9	3.00	483.00	1,139	51.3
	135	g	799	27.1	31.0	4.05	652.05	1,538	69.3
	1	c							
seeds, kernel. dry roasted	100	g	582	19.3	24.1	3.00	850.00	1,155	49.8
	32	g	186	6.2	7.7	0.96	272.00	369.60	15.9
	0.25	c							
butter, without salt added	100	g	617	17.3	23.3	3.00	576.00	666.00	55.2
	16	g	99	2.8	3.7	0.48	92.16	106.56	8.8
	1	tbsp							
oil, <60% / >60%/ >70% Linoleic	100	g	884	0.0	0.0	0.00	0.00	0.00	100.0
	13.6	g	120	0.0	0.0	0.00	0.00	0.00	13.6
	1	tbsp							
oil, industrial, mid-oleic for frying and salad dressings	100	g	884	0.0	0.0	0.00	0.00	0.00	100.0
	13.6	g	120	0.0	0.0	0.00	0.00	0.00	13.6
	1	tbsp							

PUMPKIN	SERVING QUANTITY	SERVING UNIT	CALORIES (Kcal)	PROTEIN (g)	TOTAL CARBOHYDRATES (g)	SODIUM (mg)	POTASSIUM (mg)	PHOSPHORUS (mg)	TOTAL FAT (g)
meat, 1" cubes	100	g	26	1.0	6.5	1.00	340.00	44.00	0.1
	116	g	30	1.2	7.5	1.16	394.40	51.04	0.1
	1	c							
flowers	100	g	15	1.0	3.3	5.00	173.00	49.00	0.1
	33	g	1	0.0	0.1	0.20	6.92	1.96	0.0
	1	c							
meat, boiled, drained, no salt added	100	g	20	0.7	4.9	1.00	230.00	30.00	0.1
	122.5	g	25	0.9	6.0	1.23	281.75	36.75	0.1
	0.5	c							
pumpkin pie spice powder	100	g	342	5.8	69.3	52.00	663.00	118.0	12.6
	1.7	g	6	0.1	1.2	0.88	11.27	2.01	0.2
	1	tsp							
seed sunfish, cooked dry heat	100	g	114	24.9	0.0	103.0	449.00	231.00	0.9
	85.05	g	97	21.2	0.0	87.60	381.87	196.46	0.8
	3	oz							
seeds, kernels, whole, roasted without salt added	100	g	446	18.6	53.8	18.00	919.00	92.00	19.4
	32	g	143	5.9	17.2	5.76	294.08	29.44	6.2
	0.5	c							
POPPYSEED									
oil	100	g	884	0.0	0.0	0.00	0.00	0.00	100.0
	13.6	g	120	0.0	0.0	0.00	0.00	0.00	13.6
	1	tbsp							
salad dressing, creamy	100	g	399	0.9	23.7	933.0	61.00	49.00	33.3
	33	g	132	0.3	7.8	307.9	20.13	16.17	11.0
	2	tbsp							

	SERVING QUANTITY	SERVING UNIT	CALORIES (kCal)	PROTEIN (g)	TOTAL CARBOHYDRATES (g)	SODIUM (mg)	POTASSIUM (mg)	PHOSPHORUS (mg)	TOTAL FAT (g)
OLIVE									
oil, extra virgin, virgin	100	g	884	0.0	0.0	2.00	1.00	0.00	100.0
	14	g	124	0.0	0.0	0.28	0.14	0.00	14.0
	1	tbsp							
black, kalamata	100	g	116	0.8	6.0	735.0	8.00	3.00	10.9
	15	g	17	0.1	0.9	110.0	1.20	0.45	1.6
	3	pcs							
green	100	g	145	1.0	3.8	1556	42.00	4.00	15.3
	15	g	22	0.2	0.6	233	6.30	0.60	2.3
	3	pcs							
spread (tapenade)	100	g	278	0.7	4.2	835	17.00	3.00	30.1
	16	g	45	0.1	0.7	134	2.72	0.48	4.8
	1	tbsp							
stuffed	100	g	128	1.0	4.0	1340	58.00	6.00	13.2
	15	g	19	0.2	0.6	201	8.70	0.90	2.0
	3	pcs							
COCONUT									
fresh	100	g	354	3.3	15.2	20.00	356.00	113.00	33.5
	85	g	301	2.8	12.9	17.00	303.00	96.00	28.5
	1	c							
water, unsweetened	100	g	18	0.2	4.2	26.00	165.00	5.00	0.0
	240	g	43	0.5	10.2	62.40	396.00	12.00	0.0
	1	c							
milk	100	g	31	0.2	2.9	19.00	19.00	0.00	2.1
	244	g	76	0.5	7.1	46.40	46.40	0.00	5.1
	1	c							
milk/cream for cooking	100	g	230	2.3	5.5	15.00	263.00	100.00	23.8
	240	g	552	5.5	13.3	36.00	631.00	240.00	57.2
	1	c							
yogurt	100	g	64	0.3	8.0	21.00	27.00	2.00	3.5
	170	g	109	0.5	13.5	35.70	45.90	3.40	6.0
	6	oz							
cream, canned, sweetened	100	g	357	1.2	53.2	36.00	101.00	22.00	16.3
	37	g	132	0.4	19.7	13.30	37.40	8.14	6.0
	1/4	c							
oil	100	g	833	0.0	0.0	0.00	0.00	0.00	99.1
	14	g	117	0.0	0.0	0.00	0.00	0.00	13.9
	1	tbsp							
flaked, shredded, packed	100	g	456	3.1	51.9	285.00	361.00	100.00	28.0
	28	g	128	1.0	14.5	79.80	101.00	28.00	7.8
	2	tbsp							

Fats (Oils, Nuts & Seeds)

	SERVING QUANTITY	SERVING UNIT	CALORIES (kcal)	PROTEIN (g)	TOTAL CARBOHYDRATES (g)	SODIUM (mg)	POTASSIUM (mg)	PHOSPHORUS (mg)	TOTAL FAT (g)
SAFFLOWER									
oil	100	g	884	0.0	0.0	0.00	0.00	0.00	100.0
	14	g	124	0.0	0.0	0.00	0.00	0.00	14.0
	1	tbsp							
CANOLA									
oil	100	g	884	0.0	0.0	0.00	0.00	0.00	100.0
	14	g	124	0.0	0.0	0.00	0.00	0.00	14.0
	1	tbsp							
SOYBEAN									
oil	100	g	884	0.0	0.0	0.00	0.00	0.00	100.0
	14	g	124	0.0	0.0	0.00	0.00	0.00	14.0
	1	tbsp							
BUTTER									
stick	100	g	717	0.9	0.1	643.00	24.00	24.00	81.1
	14	g	100	0.1	0.0	90.00	3.36	3.36	11.4
	1	tbsp							
light, stick or tub	100	g	499	3.3	0.0	450.00	71.00	34.00	55.1
	14	g	70	0.5	0.0	63.00	9.94	4.76	7.7
	1	tbsp							
unsalted	100	g	717	0.9	0.1	11.00	24.00	24.00	81.1
	14	g	102	0.1	0.0	1.56	3.41	3.41	11.5
	1	tbsp							
GHEE									
clarified butter	100	g	876	0.3	0.0	2.00	5.00	3.00	99.5
	14	g	123	0.0	0.0	0.28	0.70	0.42	13.9
	1	tbsp							
MARGARINE									
stick	100	g	717	0.2	0.7	751.00	18.00	5.00	80.7
	14	g	100	0.0	0.1	105.00	2.52	0.70	11.3
	1	tbsp							

G. Animal Protein

(Meats, Poultry, and Seafood)

Hey there!

Do you need to print out this Food List?

You can download a printable version of this chart by scanning the QR code below or copying the link on your computer browser.

https://go.renaltracker.com/printfoodlist

SALMON

	SERVING QUANTITY	SERVING UNIT	CALORIES (Kcal)	PROTEIN (g)	TOTAL CARBOHYDRATES (g)	SODIUM (mg)	POTASSIUM (mg)	PHOSPHORUS (mg)	TOTAL FAT (g)
pink, raw	100.00	g	127	20.5	0.0	74.99	365.96	260.98	4.40
	113.40	g	144	23.2	0.0	85.04	415.00	295.95	4.99
	4.00	oz							
atlantic, wild, raw	100.00	g	142	19.8	0.0	44.00	489.95	199.98	0.98
	113.40	g	161	22.5	0.0	49.89	555.61	226.78	1.11
	4.00	oz							
atlantic, farmed,raw	100.00	g	208	20.4	0.0	58.99	362.97	239.98	13.42
	113.39	g	236	23.2	0.0	66.90	411.60	272.13	15.22
	4.00	oz							
pink, canned, drained solids, w/ bone	100.00	g	138	23.1	0.0	380.78	332.80	378.78	5.02
	85.05	g	117	19.6	0.0	323.85	283.05	322.15	4.27
	3.00	oz							
pink, canned, with bone and liquid no salt	100.00	g	139	19.8	0.0	75.00	325.99	328.99	6.05
	56.70	g	79	11.2	0.0	42.52	184.84	186.54	3.43
	2.00	oz							
pink, canned, drained solids without skin and bones	100.00	g	136	24.6	0.0	378.00	326.00	253.00	4.21
	85.05	g	116	20.9	0.0	321.49	277.26	215.18	3.58
	3.00	oz							
chum, canned, drained, with bone no salt	100.00	g	141	21.4	0.0	75.00	300.00	353.99	5.50
	56.70	g	80	12.2	0.0	42.52	170.10	200.71	3.12
	2.00	oz							
nuggets, breaded, frozen, heated	100.00	g	212	12.7	14	173.00	165.00	176.00	11.72

TUNA

	SERVING QUANTITY	SERVING UNIT	CALORIES (Kcal)	PROTEIN (g)	TOTAL CARBOHYDRATES (g)	SODIUM (mg)	POTASSIUM (mg)	PHOSPHORUS (mg)	TOTAL FAT (g)
bluefin, raw	100.00	g	144	23.3	0.0	39.00	251.98	253.98	4.90
	113.40	g	163	26.5	0.0	44.22	285.74	288.01	5.56
	4.00	oz							
yellowfin or Ahi, raw	100.00	g	109	24.4	0.0	45.00	440.96	277.97	0.49
	113.40	g	124	27.7	0.0	51.03	500.05	315.22	0.56
	4.00	oz							
canned in oil, drained, light no salt	100.00	g	198	29.1	0.0	50.00	207.00	311.00	8.21
	56.70	g	112	16.5	0.0	28.35	117.37	176.33	4.65
	2.00	oz							
white, canned in water, drained no salt	100.00	g	128	23.6	0.0	50.00	237.00	217.00	2.97
	56.70	g	73	13.4	0.0	28.35	134.38	123.04	1.68
	2.00	oz							
canned in water, drained, light no salt	100.00	g	116	25.5	0.0	50.00	237.00	163.00	0.82
	56.70	g	66	14.5	0.0	28.35	134.38	92.42	0.46
	2.00	oz							
white, canned in oil, drained, no salt	100.00	g	186	26.5	0.0	50.00	332.99	267.00	8.08
	56.70	g	105	15.0	0.0	28.35	188.81	151.39	4.58
	2.00	oz							

	SERVING QUANTITY	SERVING UNIT	CALORIES (kcal)	PROTEIN (g)	TOTAL CARBOHYDRATES (g)	SODIUM (mg)	POTASSIUM (mg)	PHOSPHORUS (mg)	TOTAL FAT (g)
SARDINES									
spanish	100.00	g	212	6.2	14.2	310.00	0.00	na	14.16
	113.00	g	240	7.0	16.0	350.00	0.00	na	16.00
	4.00	oz							
atlantic, canned in oil, with bones	100.00	g	208	24.6	0.0	307.00	397.0	490.0	11.45
	24.00	g	50	5.9	0.0	73.68	95.28	117.6	2.75
	2.00	oz							
portuguese	100.00	g	236	25.5	0.0	500.00	na	na	12.73
	55.00	g	130	14.0	0.0	275.00	na	na	7.00
	0.50	c							
fillets, canned	100.00	g	338	18.2	7.3	364.00	na	na	26.36
	55.00	g	186	10.0	4.0	200.00	na	na	14.50
	0.25	c							
TILAPIA									
raw	100.00	g	96	20.1	0.0	52.00	302.0	170.0	1.70
	113.40	g	107	22.8	0.0	58.97	342.5	192.8	1.93
	4.00	oz							
cooked, dry heat	100.00	g	128	26.2	0.0	55.97	379.8	203.9	2.65
	85.05	g	109	22.2	0.0	47.60	323.0	173.4	2.25
	3.00	oz							
POLLOCK									
atlantic, raw	100.00	g	92	19.4	0.0	85.99	355.9	220.9	0.98
	113.40	g	104	22.0	0.0	97.51	403.7	250.6	1.11
	4.00	oz							
atlantic, cooked, dry heat	100.00	g	118	24.9	0.0	110.00	456.0	283.0	1.26
	85.05	g	100	21.2	0.0	93.55	387.8	240.7	1.07
	3.00	oz							
alaska, untreated, cooked	100.00	g	87	19.4	0.0	166.00	364.0	206.0	1.00
	85.05	g	74	16.5	0.0	141.18	309.6	175.2	0.85
	3.00	oz							
PANGASIUS (CREAM DORY/SWAI)									
fillets, boneless	100.00	g	71	14.2	0.0	186.00	na	na	1.77
	113.00	g	80	16.0	0.0	210.00	na	na	2.00
	4.00	oz							
fillets, skinless, boneless	100.00	g	177	20.4	0.0	52.00	na	na	1.77
	113.00	g	200	23.0	0.0	58.80	na	na	2.00
	4.00	oz							

	SERVING QUANTITY	SERVING UNIT	CALORIES (kcal)	PROTEIN (g)	TOTAL CARBOHYDRATES (g)	SODIUM (mg)	POTASSIUM (mg)	PHOSPHORUS (mg)	TOTAL FAT (g)
COD									
atlantic, raw	100.00	g	82	17.8	0.0	54.00	412.96	202.98	0.67
	113.40	g	93	20.2	0.0	61.23	468.30	230.18	0.76
	4.00	oz							
atlantic, canned	100.00	g	105	22.8	0.0	218.00	527.99	260.00	0.86
	56.70	g	60	12.9	0.0	123.60	299.37	147.42	0.49
	2.00	oz							
atlantic, cooked, dry heat	100.00	g	105	22.8	0.0	78.00	244.00	138.00	0.86
	85.05	g	89	19.4	0.0	66.34	207.52	117.37	0.73
	3.00	oz							
pacific, raw	100.00	g	69	15.3	0.0	302.97	234.98	280.97	0.41
	113.40	g	78	17.3	0.0	343.57	266.46	318.62	0.46
	4.00	oz							
pacific, cooked, dry heat	100.00	g	85	18.7	0.0	372.00	289.00	345.00	0.50
	85.05	g	72	15.9	0.0	316.38	245.79	293.42	0.43
	3.00	oz							
ANCHOVIES									
Raw	100.00	g	131	20.4	0.0	103.99	382.96	173.98	4.84
	113.40	g	149	23.1	0.0	117.92	434.28	197.30	5.49
	4.00	oz							
canned, in oil, drained	100.00	g	210	28.9	0.0	3,668	544.00	252.00	9.71
	16.00	g	34	4.6	0.0	586.88	87.04	40.32	1.55
	4.00	pcs							
SHRIMP									
mixed species, raw	100.00	g	71	13.6	0.9	566.00	113.00	244.00	1.01
	113.40	g	81	15.4	1.0	641.84	128.14	276.40	1.15
	4.00	oz							
mixed species, breaded, fried	100.00	g	242	21.4	12	343.80	224.87	217.87	12.27
	85.05	g	206	18.2	9.8	292.40	191.25	185.30	10.44
	3.00	oz							
mixed species, cooked, moist heat	100.00	g	119	22.8	1.5	946.99	170.00	306.00	1.70
	85.05	g	101	19.4	1.3	805.41	144.58	260.25	1.45
	3.00	oz							
cracker	100.00	g	426	7.1	59	571.00	193.00	191.00	17.86

93

	SERVING QUANTITY	SERVING UNIT	CALORIES (kcal)	PROTEIN (g)	TOTAL CARBOHYDRATES (g)	SODIUM (mg)	POTASSIUM (mg)	PHOSPHORUS (mg)	TOTAL FAT (g)
CLAMS									
mixed species, raw	100	g	86	14.7	3.6	601.00	46.00	198.00	0.96
	85.05	g	73	12.5	3.0	511.15	39.12	168.40	0.82
	3.00	oz							
mixed species, breaded, fried	100.00	g	202	14.2	10.3	364.00	326.00	188.00	11.15
	85.05	g	172	12.1	8.8	309.58	277.26	159.89	9.48
	3.00	oz							
mixed species, canned, with liquid	100.00	g	2	0.4	0.1	215.00	149.00	114.00	0.02
	28.35	g	1	0.1	0.0	60.95	42.24	32.32	0.01
	1.00	oz							
mixed species, canned, drained	100.00	g	142	24.3	5.9	112.00	627.99	326.99	1.59
	56.70	g	81	13.8	3.4	63.50	356.07	185.41	0.90
	2.00	oz							
OYSTERS									
ostrich, raw	100.00	g	125	21.6	0.0	83.00	297.00	204.00	3.67
	85.05	g	106	18.3	0.0	70.59	252.60	173.50	3.12
	3.00	oz							
ostrich, cooked	100.00	g	159	28.8	0.0	81.00	409.00	281.00	3.97
	85.05	g	135	24.5	0.0	68.89	347.85	238.99	3.38
	3.00	oz							
pacific, raw	100.00	g	81	9.5	5.0	106.00	168.00	162.00	2.30
	113.40	g	92	10.7	5.6	120.20	190.51	183.71	2.61
	4.00	oz							
pacific, cooked, moist heat	100.00	g	163	18.9	9.9	212.00	302.00	243.00	4.60
	85.05	g	139	16.1	8.4	180.30	256.85	206.67	3.91
	3.00	oz							
eastern, canned	100.00	g	68	7.1	3.9	112.00	229.00	139.00	2.47
	56.70	g	39	4.0	2.2	63.50	129.84	78.81	1.40
	2.00	oz							
eastern, farmed, raw	100.00	g	59	5.2	5.5	178.00	124.00	93.00	1.55
	85.05	g	50	4.4	4.7	151.39	105.46	79.10	1.32
	3.00	oz							
eastern, wild, raw	100.00	g	51	5.7	2.7	85.00	156.00	97.00	1.71
	113.40	g	58	6.5	3.1	96.39	176.90	110.00	1.94
	4.00	oz							
eastern, wild, breaded, fried	100.00	g	199	8.8	11.6	417.00	244.00	159.00	12.58
	85.05	g	169	7.5	9.9	354.65	207.52	135.23	10.70
	3.00	oz							
battered, breaded, fried, fast food	100.00	g	265	9.0	28.7	486.99	131.00	141.00	12.90
	85.05	g	225	7.7	24.4	414.19	111.41	119.92	10.97
	3.00	oz							

CRAB

	SERVING QUANTITY	SERVING UNIT	CALORIES (Kcal)	PROTEIN (g)	TOTAL CARBOHYDRATES (g)	SODIUM (mg)	POTASSIUM (mg)	PHOSPHORUS (mg)	TOTAL FAT (g)
blue, raw	100.0	g	87	18.1	0.0	293.00	329.00	229.00	1.08
	113.4	g	99	20.5	0.5	332.26	373.09	259.69	1.22
	4.00	oz							
blue, canned	100.0	g	83	17.9	0.0	562.99	259.00	234.00	0.74
	56.70	g	47	10.1	0.0	319.22	146.85	132.68	0.42
	2.00	oz							
dungeness, raw	100.0	g	86	17.4	0.7	295.00	354.00	182.00	0.97
	113.4	g	98	19.7	0.8	334.53	401.44	206.39	1.10
	4.00	oz							
dungeness, cooked, moist heat	100.0	g	110	22.3	1.0	378.00	408.00	175.00	1.24
	85.05	g	94	19.0	0.8	321.49	347.00	148.84	1.05
	3.00	oz							
alaska king, raw	100.0	g	84	18.3	0.0	836.00	204.00	219.00	0.60
	113.4	g	95	20.7	0.0	948.02	231.34	248.35	0.68
	4.00	oz							
alaska king, cooked, moist heat	100.0	g	97	19.4	0.0	1,072	262.00	280.00	1.54
	85.05	g	83	16.5	0.0	911.73	222.83	238.14	1.31
	3.00	oz							
imitation, crabmeat (Kani)	100.0	g	95	7.6	15.0	528.99	90.00	282.00	0.46
	85.05	g	81	6.5	12.8	449.91	76.54	239.84	0.39
	3.00	Oz							
cakes	100.0	g	266	18.8	8.5	819.00	270.00	378.00	17.25
	60.00	g	160	11.3	5.1	491.00	162.00	226.80	10.35
	1.00	pc							

CATFISH

	SERVING QUANTITY	SERVING UNIT	CALORIES (Kcal)	PROTEIN (g)	TOTAL CARBOHYDRATES (g)	SODIUM (mg)	POTASSIUM (mg)	PHOSPHORUS (mg)	TOTAL FAT (g)
channel, wild, raw	100.0	g	95	16.4	0.0	43.00	405.93	208.98	2.82
	113.4	g	108	18.6	0.0	48.76	357.97	236.98	3.20
	4.00	oz							
channel, farmed, raw	100.0	g	119	15.2	0.0	97.94	301.82	203.88	5.94
	85.05	g	101	13.0	0.0	83.30	256.70	173.40	5.05
	3.00	oz							
breaded, fried	100.0	g	229	18.1	8.0	280.00	340.00	216.00	13.33
	85.05	g	195	15.4	6.8	238.14	289.17	183.71	11.34
	3.00	oz							
wild, cooked, dry heat	100.0	g	105	18.5	0.0	50.00	419.00	304.00	2.85
	85.05	g	89	15.7	0.0	42.52	356.36	258.55	2.42
	3.00	oz							
farmed, cooked, dry heat	100.0	g	144	18.4	0.0	119.00	366.00	247.00	7.19
	85.05	g	122	15.7	0.0	101.21	311.28	210.07	6.12
	3.00	oz							

	SERVING QUANTITY	SERVING UNIT	CALORIES (kCal)	PROTEIN (g)	TOTAL CARBOHYDRATES (g)	SODIUM (mg)	POTASSIUM (mg)	PHOSPHORUS (mg)	TOTAL FAT (g)
MUSSELS									
blue, raw	100.00	g	86	11.9	3.7	286.00	320.00	197.00	2.24
	113.40	g	98	13.5	4.2	324.32	362.88	223.40	2.54
	4.00	oz							
blue, cooked, moist heat	100.00	g	172	23.8	7.4	369.00	268.00	285.00	4.48
	85.05	g	146	20.2	6.3	313.83	227.93	242.39	3.81
	3.00	oz							
atlantic or pacific, meat only	100.00	g	197	8.8	11.6	415.25	243.87	159.06	12.56
	85.05	g	167	7.5	9.9	353.17	207.41	1,315	10.69
	3.00	oz							
MACKEREL									
Atlantic or Boston, raw fillet	100.00	g	205	18.6	0.0	89.99	313.97	216.98	13.89
	113.40	g	232	21.1	0.0	102.05	356.04	246.05	15.75
	4.00	oz							
pacific and Jack, raw fillet	100.00	g	158	20.1	0.0	85.99	405.96	124.99	7.89
	113.40	g	179	22.8	0.0	97.51	460.36	141.71	8.95
	4.00	oz							
Atlantic Spanish, raw fillet	100.00	g	139	19.3	0.0	58.99	445.96	204.98	6.30
	113.40	g	158	21.9	0.0	66.90	505.71	232.45	7.14
	4.00	oz							
Jack, canned, solids, drained	100.00	g	156	23.2	0.0	378.99	194.00	301.00	6.30
	56.70	g	88	13.2	0.0	214.89	110.00	170.66	3.57
	2.00	oz							
Atlantic or Boston, cooked, dry heat	100.00	g	262	23.9	0.0	83.00	401.00	278.00	17.81
	85.05	g	223	20.3	0.0	70.59	341.05	236.44	15.15
	3.00	oz							
Atlantic, Spanish, cooked, dry heat	100.00	g	158	23.6	0.0	66.00	553.99	271.00	6.32
	85.05	g	134	20.1	0.0	56.13	471.17	230.48	5.38
	3.00	oz							
Pacific and Jack, mixed species, cooked	100.00	g	201	25.7	0.0	110.00	520.99	160.00	10.12
	85.05	g	171	21.9	0.0	93.55	443.11	136.08	8.61
	3.00	oz							

	SERVING QUANTITY	SERVING UNIT	CALORIES (kcal)	PROTEIN (g)	TOTAL CARBOHYDRATES (g)	SODIUM (mg)	POTASSIUM (mg)	PHOSPHORUS (mg)	TOTAL FAT (g)
TROUT									
rainbow, wild, raw, fillet	100.00	g	119	20.5	0.0	31.00	481.00	271.00	3.46
	113.40	g	135	23.2	0.0	35.15	545.45	307.31	3.92
	4.00	oz							
rainbow, farmed, raw, fillet	100.00	g	141	19.9	0.0	51.00	376.96	225.98	6.18
	113.40	g	160	22.6	0.0	57.83	427.48	256.26	7.01
	4.00	oz							
mixed species, raw fillet	100.00	g	148	20.8	0.0	52.00	360.97	244.98	6.61
	113.40	g	168	23.6	0.0	58.96	409.33	277.80	7.50
	4.00	oz							
sea trout, mixed species, raw	100.00	g	104	16.7	0.0	57.99	340.97	249.98	3.61
	113.40	g	118	19.0	0.0	65.77	386.66	283.47	4.09
	4.00	oz							
rainbow, wild, cooked, dry heat	100.00	g	150	22.9	0.0	56.00	448.00	269.00	5.82
	85.05	g	128	19.5	0.0	47.63	381.02	228.78	4.95
	3.00	oz							
rainbow, farmed, cooked, dry heat	100.00	g	168	23.8	0.0	61.00	450.00	270.00	7.38
	85.05	g	143	20.2	0.0	51.88	382.72	229.63	6.28
	3.00	oz							
mixed species, cooked, dry heat	100.00	g	190	26.6	0.0	67.00	463.00	314.00	8.47
	85.05	g	162	22.7	0.0	56.98	393.78	267.05	7.20
	3.00	oz							
sea trout, mixed species, cooked, dry heat	100.00	g	133	21.5	0.0	74.00	437.00	321.00	4.63
	85.05	g	113	18.3	0.0	62.94	371.66	273.01	3.94
	3.00	oz							
CARP									
raw	100.00	g	127	17.8	0.0	49.00	332.97	414.96	5.60
	113.40	g	144	20.2	0.0	55.56	377.59	470.56	6.35
	4.00	oz							
cooked, dry heat	100.00	g	162	22.9	0.0	63.00	427.00	530.99	7.17
	85.05	g	138	19.4	0.0	53.58	363.16	451.61	6.10
	3.00	oz							
MAHI-MAHI									
Dorado or Dolphinfish, raw	100.00	g	85	18.5	0.0	87.99	415.96	142.99	0.70
	113.40	g	96	21.0	0.0	99.78	471.70	162.15	0.79
	4.00	oz							
Doradao or Dolphinfish, cooked, dry heat	100.00	g	109	23.7	0.0	113.00	532.99	183.00	0.90
	85.05	g	93	20.2	0.0	96.11	452.31	155.64	0.77
	3.00	oz							

	SERVING QUANTITY	SERVING UNIT	CALORIES (kcal)	PROTEIN (g)	TOTAL CARBOHYDRATES (g)	SODIUM (mg)	POTASSIUM (mg)	PHOSPHORUS (mg)	TOTAL FAT (g)
FLATFISH									
raw	100.00	g	70	12.4	0.0	295.97	159.98	251.98	1.93
	113.40	g	79	14.1	0.0	335.63	181.42	285.74	2.19
	4.00	oz							
cooked, dry heat	100.00	g	86	15.2	0.0	363.00	197.00	309.00	2.37
	85.05	g	73	13.0	0.0	308.73	167.55	262.80	2.02
	3.00	oz							
HALIBUT									
greenland, raw	100.00	g	186	14.4	0.0	79.99	267.97	163.98	13.84
	113.40	g	211	16.3	0.0	90.71	303.88	185.96	15.69
	4.00	oz							
atlantic and pacific, raw	100.00	g	91	18.6	0.0	67.99	434.96	235.98	1.33
	113.40	g	103	21.0	0.0	77.10	493.24	267.60	1.51
	4.00	oz							
greenland, cooked, dry heat	100.00	g	239	18.4	0.0	103.00	344.00	210.00	17.71
	85.05	g	203	15.7	0.0	87.60	292.57	178.60	15.09
	3.00	oz							
atlantic and pacific, cooked, dry heat	100.00	g	111	22.5	0.0	82.00	527.99	287.00	1.61
	85.05	g	94	19.2	0.0	69.74	449.06	244.09	1.37
	3.00	oz							
LOBSTER									
Northern, raw (Langoustine)	100.00	g	77	16.5	0.0	423.00	200.00	161.00	0.75
	113.40	g	87	18.7	0.0	479.68	226.80	182.57	0.85
	4.00	Oz							
Spiny, mixed species, raw	100.00	g	112	20.6	2.4	177.00	180.00	238.00	1.51
	113.40	g	127	23.4	2.8	200.72	104.12	269.89	1.71
	4.00	oz							
Northern, cooked, moist heat (Langoustine)	100.00	g	89	19.0	0.0	485.99	230.00	185.00	0.86
	85.05	g	76	16.2	0.0	413.34	195.61	157.34	0.73
	3.00	oz							
Spiny, mixed species, cooked, moist heat	100.00	g	143	26.4	3.1	227.00	208.00	229.00	1.94
	85.05	g	122	22.5	2.7	193.06	176.90	194.76	1.65
	3.00	oz							

	SERVING QUANTITY	SERVING UNIT	CALORIES (kcal)	PROTEIN (g)	TOTAL CARBOHYDRATES (g)	SODIUM (mg)	POTASSIUM (mg)	PHOSPHORUS (mg)	TOTAL FAT (g)
SCALLOPS									
Mixed species, raw	100.00	g	69	12.1	3.2	392.00	205.00	12.80	0.49
	113.40	g	78	13.7	3.6	444.53	232.47	14.52	0.56
	4.00	oz							
Bay and Sea, steamed	100.00	g	111	20.5	5.4	667.00	314.00	426.00	0.84
	85.05	g	94	17.5	4.6	567.28	267.06	362.31	0.71
	3.00	oz							
mixed species, breaded and fried	100.00	g	216	18.1	10.1	464.00	333.00	236.00	10.94
	46.50	g	100	8.4	4.7	215.76	15.85	109.74	5.09
	3.00	pcs							
breaded, fried, fast food	100.00	g	268	10.9	26.7	637.99	204.00	203.00	13.47
	85.05	g	228	9.3	22.7	542.61	173.50	172.65	11.46
	3.00	oz							
HERRING									
Pacific, raw	100.00	g	195	16.4	0.0	73.99	422.96	227.98	13.88
	113.40	g	221	18.6	0.0	83.91	479.64	258.53	15.74
	4.00	oz							
Atlantic, raw	100.00	g	158	18.0	0.0	89.99	326.97	235.98	9.04
	113.40	g	179	20.4	0.0	102.05	370.78	267.60	10.25
	4.00	oz							
Pacific, cooked, dry heat	100.00	g	250	21.0	0.0	95.00	541.99	292.00	17.79
	85.05	g	213	17.9	0.0	80.80	460.97	248.34	15.13
	3.00	oz							
Atlantic, cooked, dry heat	100.00	g	203	23.0	0.0	115.00	419.00	303.00	11.49
	85.05	g	173	19.6	0.0	97.81	356.36	257.70	9.86
	3.00	oz							
Roe or eggs, Pacific (Alaska Native)	100.00	g	74	9.6	4.5	61.00	na	na	1.93
	85.05	g	63	8.2	3.8	51.88	na	na	1.64
	3.00	oz							

CRAYFISH/ CRAWFISH	SERVING QUANTITY	SERVING UNIT	CALORIES (kcal)	PROTEIN (g)	TOTAL CARBOHYDRATES (g)	SODIUM (mg)	POTASSIUM (mg)	PHOSPHORUS (mg)	TOTAL FAT (g)
Mixed species, farmed, raw	100.00	g	72	14.9	0.0	62.00	261.00	218.00	0.97
	113.40 4.00	g oz	82	16.8	0.0	70.31	295.97	247.21	1.10
Mixed species, wild, raw	100.00	g	77	16.0	0.0	58.00	302.00	256.00	0.95
	113.40 4.00	g oz	87	18.1	0.0	65.77	342.47	290.30	1.08
Mixed species, farmed, cooked, moist heat	100.00	g	87	17.5	0.0	97.00	238.00	241.00	0.22
	85.05 3.00	g oz	74	14.9	0.0	82.50	202.42	204.97	0.18
mixed species, wild, cooked, moist heat	100.00	g	82	16.8	0.0	94.00	296.00	270.00	1.20
	85.05 3.00	g oz	70	14.3	0.0	79.95	251.75	229.63	1.02
SQUID (CALAMARI)									
mixed species, fried	100.00	g	175	17.9	7.8	306.0	279.00	251.00	7.48
	85.05 3.00	g oz	149	15.3	6.6	260.3	237.29	213.47	6.36
mixed species, raw boneless	100.00	g	92	15.6	3.1	44.00	246.00	221.00	1.38
	113.40 4.00	g oz	104	17.7	3.5	49.90	278.96	250.61	1.56

EGG

	SERVING QUANTITY	SERVING UNIT	CALORIES (Kcal)	PROTEIN (g)	TOTAL CARBOHYDRATES (g)	SODIUM (mg)	POTASSIUM (mg)	PHOSPHORUS (mg)	TOTAL FAT (g)
chicken, raw, large	100.00	g	143	12.6	0.7	142.00	138.00	198.00	9.51
	50.00	g	72	6.3	0.4	71.00	69.00	99.00	4.76
	1.00	pc							
chicken, fried, large	100.00	g	196	13.6	0.8	207.00	152.00	215.00	14.84
	46.00	g	90	6.3	0.4	95.22	69.92	98.90	6.83
	1.00	pc							
chicken, poached, large	100.00	g	143	12.5	0.7	297.00	138.00	197.00	9.47
	50.00	g	72	6.3	0.4	148.50	69.00	98.50	4.74
	1.00	pc							
chicken, hard boiled, large	100.00	g	155	12.6	1.1	124.00	126.00	172.00	10.61
	50.00	g	78	6.3	0.6	62.00	63.00	86.00	5.31
	1.00	pc							
scrambled, fast food	100.00	g	212	13.8	2.1	187.00	147.00	242.00	16.18
	94.00	g	199	13.0	2.0	175.78	138.18	227.48	15.21
	2.00	pc							
substitute, liquid	100.00	g	84	12.0	0.6	177.00	330.00	121.00	3.31
	251.00	g	211	30.1	1.6	444.27	828.30	303.71	8.31
	1.00	c							
substitute, powder	100.00	g	443	55.8	22	798.19	742.31	476.92	12.97
	9.92	g	44	5.5	2.2	79.20	73.66	47.32	1.29
	0.35	oz							
substitute, frozen	100.00	g	160	11.3	3.2	199.00	213.00	72.00	11.11
	60.00	g	96	6.8	1.9	119.40	127.80	43.20	6.67
	0.25	c							
chicken, egg whites only, raw large egg	100.00	g	52	10.9	0.7	166.00	163.00	15.00	0.17
	33.00	g	17	3.6	0.2	54.78	53.79	4.95	0.06
	1.00	pc							
chicken, yolk only, raw large egg	100.00	g	322	15.9	3.6	48.00	109.00	390.00	26.54
	17.00	g	55	2.7	0.6	8.16	18.53	66.30	4.51
	1.00	pc							
chicken, whole, raw, frozen	100.00	g	147	12.3	1.0	128.00	135.00	193.00	9.95
	56.70	g	83	7.0	0.6	72.57	76.54	109.43	5.64
	2.00	oz							
yolk only, frozen, raw	100.00	g	296	15.5	0.8	67.00	121.00	419.99	25.60
	56.70	g	168	8.8	0.5	37.99	68.61	238.14	14.51
	2.00	oz							
whites, frozen, raw	100.00	g	48	10.2	1.0	169.00	169.00	13.00	0.00
	56.70	g	27	5.8	0.6	95.82	95.82	7.37	0.00
	2.00	oz							
duck, raw	100.00	g	185	12.8	1.5	146.00	222.00	220.00	13.77
	70.00	g	130	9.0	1.0	102.20	155.40	154.00	9.64
	1.00	pc							
quail, raw	100.00	g	158	13.1	0.4	141.00	132.00	226.00	11.09
	9.00	g	14	1.2	0.0	12.69	11.88	20.34	1.00
	1.00	pc							

CHICKEN

	SERVING QUANTITY	SERVING UNIT	CALORIES (kcal)	PROTEIN (g)	TOTAL CARBOHYDRATES (g)	SODIUM (mg)	POTASSIUM (mg)	PHOSPHORUS (mg)	TOTAL FAT (g)
ground, raw	100.00	g	143	17.4	0.0	60.00	522.00	178.00	8.10
meat and skin, raw	100.00	g	215	18.6	0.0	70.00	189.00	147.00	15.06
	113.40	g	244	21.1	0.0	79.38	214.33	166.70	17.08
	4.00	oz							
meat and skin, roasted	100.00	g	239	27.3	0.0	82.00	223.00	182.00	13.60
	85.05	g	203	23.2	0.0	69.74	189.66	154.79	11.57
	3.00	oz							
thigh meat only, fried	100.00	g	218	28.2	1.2	95.00	259.00	199.00	10.30
	85.05	g	185	24.0	1.0	80.80	220.28	169.25	8.76
	3.00	oz							
thigh meat only, roasted	100.00	g	179	24.8	0.0	106.00	269.00	230.00	8.15
	85.05	g	152	21.1	0.0	90.15	228.78	195.61	6.93
	3.00	oz							
wing meat only, fried	100.00	g	211	30.2	0.0	91.00	208.00	164.00	9.15
	85.05	g	179	25.6	0.0	77.39	176.90	139.48	7.78
	3.00	oz							
wing meat only, roasted	100.00	g	203	30.5	0.0	92.00	210.00	166.00	8.13
	85.05	g	173	26.0	0.0	78.25	178.60	141.18	6.91
	3.00	oz							
wing meat only, stewed	100.00	g	181	27.2	0.0	73.00	153.00	134.00	7.18
	85.05	g	154	23.1	0.0	62.09	130.12	113.97	6.11
	3.00	oz							
back meat only, fried	100.00	g	288	30.0	5.7	99.00	251.00	176.00	4.12
	85.05	g	245	25.5	4.8	84.20	213.47	149.69	3.50
	3.00	oz							
back meat only, roasted	100.00	g	239	28.2	0.0	96.00	237.00	165.00	13.16
	85.05	g	203	24.0	0.0	81.65	201.57	140.33	11.19
	3.00	oz							
back meat only, stewed	100.00	g	209	25.3	0.0	67.00	158.00	130.00	11.19
	85.05	g	178	21.5	0.0	56.98	134.38	110.56	9.52
	3.00	oz							
drumstick meat only, fried	100.00	g	195	28.6	0.0	96.00	249.00	186.00	8.08
	85.05	g	166	24.3	0.0	81.65	211.77	158.19	6.87
	3.00	oz							
drumstick meat only, roasted	100.00	g	155	24.2	0.0	128.00	256.00	200.00	5.70
	85.05	g	132	20.6	0.0	108.86	217.73	170.10	4.85
	3	oz							

CHICKEN

	SERVING QUANTITY	SERVING UNIT	CALORIES (kcal)	PROTEIN (g)	TOTAL CARBOHYDRATES (g)	SODIUM (mg)	POTASSIUM (mg)	PHOSPHORUS (mg)	TOTAL FAT (g)
drumstick meat only, stewed	100.00	g	169	27.5	0.0	80.00	199.00	150.00	5.71
	85.05 3.00	g oz	144	23.4	0.0	68.04	169.25	127.57	4.86
leg meat only, fried	100.00	g	208	28.4	0.7	96.00	254.00	193.00	9.32
	85.05 3.00	g oz	177	24.1	0.6	81.65	216.02	164.14	7.93
leg meat only, roasted	100.00	g	174	24.2	0.0	99.00	269.00	205.00	7.80
	85.05 3.00	g oz	148	20.6	0.0	84.20	228.78	174.35	6.63
leg meat only, stewed	100.00	g	185	26.3	0.0	78.00	190.00	149.00	8.06
	85.05 3.00	g oz	157	22.3	0.0	66.34	161.59	126.72	6.85
pate, chicken liver, canned	100.00	g	201	13.5	6.6	386.0	95.00	175.00	13.10
	52.00 4.00	g tbsp	105	7.0	3.4	200.7	49.40	91.00	6.81
chicken tenders, fast food	100.00	g	271	19.2	17.3	769.0	373.00	282.00	13.95
	62.00 4.00	g pcs	168	11.9	10.7	476.8	231.26	174.84	8.65
chicken patty, frozen, cooked	100.00	g	287	14.9	12.8	532.0	261.00	208.00	19.58
bratwurst, chicken, cooked	100.00	g	176	19.4	0.0	72.00	211.00	160.00	10.30
	83.92 2.96	g oz	148	16.3	0.0	60.42	177.06	134.27	8.69
sausage, chicken/beef, smoked	100.00	g	295	18.5	0.0	1,020	139.00	111.00	244.00
	138.00 1.00	g c	251	15.7	0.0	867.5	118.22	94.41	20.41

TURKEY	SERVING QUANTITY	SERVING UNIT	CALORIES (kCal)	PROTEIN (g)	TOTAL CARBOHYDRATES (g)	SODIUM (mg)	POTASSIUM (mg)	PHOSPHORUS (mg)	TOTAL FAT (g)
breast, meat &	100.00	g	144	21.6	0.1	112.00	224.00	183.00	5.64
skin, raw	113.40	g	163	24.5	0.2	127.01	254.02	207.52	6.40
	4.00	oz							
breast, meat &	100.00	g	189	28.6	0.1	103.00	239.00	223.00	7.39
skin, roasted	85.05	g	161	24.3	0.1	87.60	203.27	189.66	6.29
	3.00	oz							
breast, meat	100.00	g	114	23.3	0.0	74.00	267.00	185.00	2.33
only, raw	85.05	g	97	19.9	0.0	62.94	227.08	157.34	1.98
	3.00	oz							
breast, meat	100.00	g	136	29.5	0.0	114.00	297.00	253.00	1.97
only, roasted	85.05	g	116	25.1	0.0	96.96	252.60	215.17	1.68
	3.00	oz							
ground, raw	100.00	g	148	20.0	0.0	58.00	237.00	200.00	7.66
	113.40	g	168	22.3	0.0	65.77	268.76	226.80	8.69
	4.00	oz							
ground,	100.00	g	203	27.4	0.0	78.00	294.00	254.00	10.40
cooked	85.05	g	173	23.3	0.0	66.34	250.04	216.02	8.85
	3.00	oz							
white	100.00	g	112	13.5	7.7	1,200	349.00	158.00	3.00
rotisserie, deli	56.70	g	64	7.7	4.4	680.40	197.88	89.59	1.70
cut	2.00	oz							
ham, extra	100.00	g	134	19.6	0.9	1,038	299.00	304.00	5.80
lean, sliced	20.00	g	27	3.9	0.2	207.60	59.80	60.80	1.16
	1.00	pc							
pastrami,	100.00	g	139	16.3	3.3	1,123	345.00	200.00	6.21
sliced	56.70	g	79	9.2	1.9	636.74	195.62	113.40	3.52
	2.00	slices							
bologna	100.00	g	209	11.4	4.7	1,071	135.00	114.00	16.05
	56.70	g	119	6.5	2.7	607.26	76.55	64.64	9.10
	2.00	slices							
salami	100.00	g	172	19.2	1.6	1,107	216.00	266.00	9.21
	56.70	g	98	10.9	0.9	627.67	122.47	150.82	5.22
	2.00	slices							
bacon, turkey,	100.00	g	382	29.6	3.1	2,285	395.00	460.00	27.90
cooked	28.35	g	108	8.4	0.9	647.80	111.98	130.41	7.91
	1.00	oz							
bacon, turkey,	100.00	g	253	13.3	4.8	900.00	156.00	145.00	20.00
low sodium	15.00	g	38	2.0	0.7	135.00	23.40	21.75	3.00
	1.00	svg							
sausage,	100.00	g	196	23.9	0.0	665.00	298.00	202.00	10.44
turkey, cooked	56.70	g	111	13.6	0.0	377.06	168.97	114.53	5.92
	2.00	oz							

PORK	SERVING QUANTITY	SERVING UNIT	CALORIES (kcal)	PROTEIN (g)	TOTAL CARBOHYDRATES (g)	SODIUM (mg)	POTASSIUM (mg)	PHOSPHORUS (mg)	TOTAL FAT (g)
ground, cooked	100.00	g	297	25.7	0.0	73.00	362.00	226.00	20.77
	85.05	g	253	21.9	0.0	62.09	307.88	192.21	17.66
	3.00	oz							
ground, raw	100.00	g	263	16.9	0.0	56.00	287.00	175.00	21.19
	113.40	g	298	19.1	0.0	63.50	325.46	198.45	24.03
	4.00	oz							
loin, sirloin, roasts, separable lean roasted	100.00	g	204	27.8	0.0	59.00	352.00	235.00	9.44
	85.05	g	174	23.6	0.0	50.18	299.37	199.87	8.03
	3.00	oz							
loin, center rib, separable lean, roasted	100.00	g	206	28.8	0.0	95.00	287.00	244.00	9.21
	85.05	g	175	24.5	0.0	80.80	244.09	207.52	7.83
	3.00	oz							
loin, sirloin, boneless, separable lean roasted	100.00	g	178	30.4	0.0	66.00	408.00	311.00	5.31
	85.05	g	151	25.9	0.0	56.13	347.00	264.50	4.52
	3.00	oz							
loin, center rib, boneless roasted	100.00	g	214	28.8	0.0	50.00	363.00	222.00	10.13
	85.05	g	182	24.5	0.0	42.52	308.73	188.81	8.62
	3.00	oz							
shoulder blade, boston roasts roasted turkey, salt.	100.00	g	232	24.2	0.0	88.00	427.00	235.00	14.30
	85.05	g	197	20.6	0.0	74.84	363.16	199.87	12.16
	3.00	oz							
shoulder, whole, roasted	100.00	g	230	25.3	0.0	74.96	345.80	220.87	13.53
	85.05	g	196	21.5	0.0	63.75	294.10	187.85	11.51
	3.00	oz							
loin, whole, roasted	100.00	g	209	28.6	0.0	58.00	425.00	249.00	9.63
	85.05	g	178	24.3	0.0	49.33	361.46	211.77	8.19
	3.00	oz							
leg or ham, whole, roasted	100.00	g	211	29.4	0.0	64.00	373.00	281.00	9.44
	85.05	g	179	25.0	0.0	54.43	317.23	238.99	8.03
	3.00	oz							
loin, tenderloin, separable lean & fat roasted	100.00	g	147	26.0	0.0	57.00	419.00	265.00	3.96
	85.05	g	125	22.2	0.0	48.48	356.36	225.38	3.37
	3.00	oz							
ground, cooked	100.00	g	297	25.7	0.0	73.00	362.00	226.00	20.77
	85.05	g	253	21.9	0.0	62.09	307.88	192.21	17.66
	3.00	oz							

PORK	SERVING QUANTITY	SERVING UNIT	CALORIES (kCal)	PROTEIN (g)	TOTAL CARBOHYDRATES (g)	SODIUM (mg)	POTASSIUM (mg)	PHOSPHORUS (mg)	TOTAL FAT (g)
bacon, cured, broiled, panfried or roasted	100.00	g	541	37.0	1.4	1,717.0	565.0	533.0	41.78
	8.00	g	43	3.0	0.1	137.36	45.20	42.64	3.34
	1.00	slice							
bacon, reduced sodium, cured broiled, panfried or roasted	100.00	g	541	37.0	1.4	1,030.0	565.0	533.0	41.78
	56.70	g	307	21.0	0.8	584.01	320.4	302.2	23.69
	2.00	oz							
country style ribs, separable lean & fat roasted	100.00	g	359	21.8	0.0	52.00	322.0	214.0	29.46
	85.05	g	305	18.5	0.0	44.23	273.9	182.0	25.06
	3.00	oz							
sirloin, chops or roasts, boneless, raw	100.00	g	121	22.8	0.0	63.00	354.0	251.0	2.59
	113.40	g	137	25.9	0.0	71.44	401.4	284.6	2.94
	4.00	oz							
kidney, braised	100.00	g	151	25.4	0.0	80.00	143.0	240.0	4.70
	85.05	g	128	21.6	0.0	68.04	121.6	204.1	4.00
	3.00	oz							
liver, braised	100.00	g	165	26.0	3.8	49.00	150.0	241.0	4.40
	85.05	g	140	22.1	3.2	41.67	127.6	205.0	3.74
	3.00	oz							
ham, minced, sliced	100.00	g	263	16.3	1.8	1,245.0	311.0	157.0	20.68
	21.00	g	55	3.4	0.4	261.45	65.31	32.97	4.34
	1.00	slice							
ham, extra lean, 5% fat	100.00	g	107	16.9	0.7	944.99	463.0	252.0	4.04
	85.05	g	91	14.3	0.6	803.71	393.8	214.3	3.44
	3.00	oz							
ham, low sodium, cured, cooked	100.00	g	165	22.0	0.5	969.00	362.0	248.0	7.70
	85.05	g	140	18.7	0.4	824.13	307.9	210.9	6.55
	3.00	oz							
sausages, Kielbasa, grilled	100.00	g	337	12.5	5.0	1,062	306.0	204.0	29.68
	85.05	g	287	10.6	4.3	903.22	260.3	173.5	25.24
	3.00	oz							
Kielbasa, panfried	100.00	g	333	12.4	4.8	1,046	304.0	199.0	29.43
	85.05	g	283	10.5	4.1	889.61	258.6	169.3	25.03
	3.00	oz							
Beerwurst, pork/beef	100.00	g	276	14.0	4.3	732.00	244.0	135.0	22.53
	56.70	g	156	7.9	2.4	415.04	138.4	76.6	12.77
	2.00	oz							

PORK

	SERVING QUANTITY	SERVING UNIT	CALORIES (kcal)	PROTEIN (g)	TOTAL CARBOHYDRATES (g)	SODIUM (mg)	POTASSIUM (mg)	PHOSPHORUS (mg)	TOTAL FAT (g)
Italian Sweet, links	100	g	149	16.1	2.1	570.00	194.00	103.00	8.42
	85.05 3	g oz	127	13.7	1.8	484.79	165.00	87.60	7.16
Polish, pork, cooked	100	g	326	14.1	1.6	875.99	237.00	136.00	28.72
	56.70 2	g oz	185	8.0	0.9	496.68	134.38	77.11	16.28
Bratwurst, pork, cooked	100	g	333	13.7	2.9	845.99	347.99	208.00	29.18
	56.70 2	g oz	189	7.8	1.6	479.67	197.31	117.93	16.54
meatloaf/ luncheon meat pork/beef	100	g	260	15.4	1.6	1,182	245.00	122.00	20.90
	2 1	g slice	60	3.5	0.4	271.86	56.35	28.06	4.81
peperoni, beef/pork	100	g	504	19.3	1.2	1,582	274.00	158.00	46.28
	56.70 2	g oz	286	11.0	0.7	896.98	155.36	89.58	26.24
salami, italian, pork	100	g	425	21.7	1.2	1,890	340.00	229.00	37.00
	28.35 1	g oz	120	6.2	0.3	535.82	96.39	64.92	10.49

BEEF	SERVING QUANTITY	SERVING UNIT	CALORIES (kcal)	PROTEIN (g)	TOTAL CARBOHYDRATES (g)	SODIUM (mg)	POTASSIUM (mg)	PHOSPHORUS (mg)	TOTAL FAT (g)
chuck eyeroast, boneless, all grades 0" fat, separable lean only, **roasted**	3	g	183	26.7	0.0	68.04	344.00	210.00	8.46
	85.05	g	156	22.7	0.0	80.00	292.57	178.61	7.20
	3.00	oz							
chuck eyeroast, boneless, all grades separable lean only, 0", **raw**	100.00	g	137	20.6	0.0	85.00	357.00	204.00	6.01
	85.05	g	117	17.5	0.0	72.29	303.63	173.50	5.11
	3.00	oz							
chuck eyeroast, boneless, all grades sep lean & fat, 0" fat, **roasted**	100.00	g	236	24.6	0.0	76.00	308.00	187.00	15.29
	85.05	g	201	21.0	0.0	64.64	261.95	159.04	13.00
	3.00	oz							
chuck eyeroast, boneless, all grades sep lean & fat, 0" fat, **raw**	100.00	g	173	19.3	0.0	82.00	367.00	187.00	10.67
	85.05	g	147	16.4	0.0	69.74	312.13	159.04	9.07
	3.00	oz							
jerky	100.00	g	410	33.2	11	1,785	597.00	407.00	25.60
	28.35	g	116	9.4	3.1	506.05	169.25	115.38	7.26
	1.00	oz							
corned beef, brisket, **raw**	100.00	g	198	14.7	0.1	1,217	297.00	117.00	14.90
	113.40	g	225	16.7	0.2	1,380	336.80	132.68	16.90
	4.00	oz							
corned beef, brisket, **cooked**	100.00	g	251	18.2	0.5	927.99	145.00	125.00	18.98
	85.05	g	213	15.5	0.4	827.53	123.32	106.31	16.14
	3.00	oz							
broth cube 1 cube, 6 fl. oz prepared	100.00	g	170	17.3	16	24,000	403.00	225.00	4.00
	3.60	g	6	0.6	0.6	864.00	14.51	8.10	0.14
	1.00	cube							
liver, pan fried	100.00	g	175	26.5	5.2	77.00	351.00	485.00	4.68
	81.00	g	142	21.5	4.2	62.37	284.31	392.85	3.79
	1.00	slice							
liver, braised	100.00	g	191	29.1	5.1	79.00	352.00	496.99	5.26
	85.05	g	162	24.7	4.4	67.19	299.37	422.69	4.47
	3.00	oz							
tongue, simmered	100.00	g	284	19.3	0.0	65.00	184.00	145.00	22.30
	85.05	g	242	16.4	0.0	55.28	156.49	123.32	18.97
	3.00	oz							
kidney simmered	100.00	g	158	27.3	0.0	94.00	135.00	304.00	4.65
	85.05	g	134	23.2	0.0	79.95	114.82	258.55	3.95
	3.00	oz							
tripe, simmered	100.00	g	94	11.7	2.0	68.00	42.00	66.00	4.05
	85.05	g	80	10.0	1.7	57.83	35.72	56.13	3.44
	3.00	oz							

	SERVING QUANTITY	SERVING UNIT	CALORIES (kcal)	PROTEIN (g)	TOTAL CARBOHYDRATES (g)	SODIUM (mg)	POTASSIUM (mg)	PHOSPHORUS (mg)	TOTAL FAT (g)
LAMB									
tenderloin, New Zealand, separable lean only, *raw*	100.00	g	116	20.5	0.0	49.00	381.00	222.00	3.81
	85.05	g	99	17.5	0.0	41.67	324.04	188.81	3.24
	3.00	oz							
loin, NZ, separable lean, frozen, **broiled**	100.00	g	199	29.3	0.0	55.00	189.00	240.00	8.24
	85.05	g	169	24.9	0.0	46.78	160.74	204.12	7.01
	3.00	oz							
australian, separable lean, 1/8" fat, **cooked**	100.00	g	201	26.7	0.0	80.00	318.00	207.00	9.63
	85.05	g	171	22.7	0.0	68.04	270.46	176.05	8.19
	3.00	oz							
Australian, separable lean, 1/8" fat, *raw*	100.00	g	142	20.3	0.0	83.00	320.00	188.00	6.18
	113.40	g	161	23.0	0.0	94.12	362.88	213.19	7.01
	4.00	oz							
Australian, ground, 85%Lean/15%fat, raw	100.00	g	255	17.1	0.0	65.49	na	na	20.17
	85.05	g	217	14.6	0.0	77.00	na	na	17.61
	3.00	oz							
NZ, rib, separable lean, frozen, *raw*	100.00	g	160	20.7	0.0	67.00	309.00	185.00	8.61
	113.40	g	181	23.4	0.0	75.98	350.41	209.79	9.76
	4.00	oz							
NZ, rib, separable lean, frozen, roasted	100.00	g	193	24.4	0.0	72.00	323.00	209.00	10.63
	85.05	g	164	20.8	0.0	61.24	274.71	177.75	9.04
	3.00	oz							
VEAL									
separable lean, cooked	100.00	g	196	32.0	0.0	89.00	338.00	250.00	6.58
	85.05	g	167	27.1	0.0	75.69	287.47	212.62	5.60
	3.00	oz							
liver, pan fried	100.00	g	193	27.4	4.5	85.00	353.00	482.99	6.51
	85.05	g	164	23.3	3.8	72.29	300.22	410.79	5.54
	3.00	oz							
sausage, bratwurst, veal, cooked	100.00	g	341	14.0	0.0	60.00	231.00	150.00	31.70
	83.92	g	286	11.7	0.0	50.35	193.85	125.87	26.60
	2.96	oz							
ground, pan fried	100.00	g	503	8.9	0.9	89.00	107.00	133.00	51.60
	85.05	g	428	7.5	0.8	75.69	91.00	113.12	43.89
	3.00	oz							

VEAL	SERVING QUANTITY	SERVING UNIT	CALORIES (kCal)	PROTEIN (g)	TOTAL CARBOHYDRATES (g)	SODIUM (mg)	POTASSIUM (mg)	PHOSPHORUS (mg)	TOTAL FAT (g)
sirloin, separable, lean, braised	100.00	g	204	34.0	0.0	81.00	339.00	259.00	6.51
	85.05	g	174	28.9	0.0	68.89	288.32	220.28	5.54
	3.00	oz							
sirloin separable lean, roasted	100.00	g	168	26.3	0.0	85.00	365.00	231.00	6.22
	85.05	g	143	22.4	0.0	72.29	310.43	196.46	5.29
	3.00	oz							
sirloin, lean, raw	100.00	g	110	20.2	0.0	80.00	348.00	220.00	2.59
	113.40	g	125	22.9	0.0	90.72	394.63	249.48	2.94
	4.00	oz							
loin, lean and fat, braised	100.00	g	284	30.2	0.0	80.00	280.00	220.00	17.21
	85.05	g	242	25.7	0.0	68.04	238.14	187.11	14.64
	3.00	oz							
loin, lean and fat, roasted	100.00	g	217	25.0	0.0	93.00	325.00	212.00	12.32
	85.05	g	185	21.1	0.0	79.10	276.41	180.30	10.48
	3.00	oz							
loin, lean, braised	100.00	g	226	33.6	0.0	84.00	297.00	237.00	9.15
	85.05	g	192	28.6	0.0	71.44	252.60	201.57	7.78
	3.00	oz							
loin, lean, roasted	100.00	g	175	26.3	0.0	96.00	340.00	222.00	6.94
	85.05	g	149	22.4	0.0	81.65	289.17	188.81	5.90
	3.00	oz							
loin, lean, raw	100.00	g	114	21.9	0.0	99.00	260.00	237.00	2.90
	113.40	g	129	24.8	0.0	112.27	294.84	268.76	3.29
	4.00	oz							
loin, chop, lean and fat, grilled	100.00	g	198	28.0	0.2	86.00	229.00	208.00	9.48
	85.05	g	168	23.9	0.1	73.14	194.76	176.90	8.06
	3.00	oz							
bratwwurst, veal, cooked	100.00	g	341	14.0	0.0	60.00	231.00	150.00	31.70
	83.92	g	286	11.7	0.0	50.35	193.85	125.87	26.60
	2.96	oz							

H. Herbs and Spices

Hey there!

Do you need to print out this Food List?

You can download a printable version of this chart by scanning the QR code below or copying the link on your computer browser.

https://go.renaltracker.com/printfoodlist

	SERVING QUANTITY	SERVING UNIT	CALORIES (kcal)	PROTEIN (g)	TOTAL CARBOHYDRATES (g)	SODIUM (mg)	POTASSIUM (mg)	PHOSPHORUS (mg)	TOTAL FAT (g)
ONION									
red, raw	100	g	44	0.94	9.93	1	197	41	0.1
1 onion	197	g	86.7	1.85	19.6	1.97	388	80.8	0.197
white, raw	100	g	36	0.89	7.68	2	141	29	0.13
yellow, raw	100	g	38	0.83	8.61	1	182	34	0.05
1 onion	143	g	54.3	1.19	12.3	1.43	260	48.6	0.071
GARLIC									
raw	100	g	149	6.36	33.1	17	401	153	0.5
3 cloves	9	g	13.4	0.572	2.98	1.53	36.1	13.8	0.045
GINGER									
raw	100	g	80	1.82	17.8	13	415	34	0.75
SPRING ONIONS									
raw	100	g	32	1.83	7.34	16	276	37	0.19
1 large	25	g	8	0.458	1.84	4	69	9.25	0.048
CHIVES									
raw	100	g	30	3.27	4.35	3	296	58	0.73
BASIL									
fresh	100	g	23	3.15	2.65	4	295	56	0.64
dried	100	g	233	23	47.8	76	2630	274	4.07
OREGANO									
dried	100	g	265	9	68.9	25	1260	148	4.28
ROSEMARY									
fresh	100	g	131	3.31	20.7	26	668	66	5.86
dried	100	g	331	4.88	64.1	50	995	70	15.2
MARJORAM									
dried	100	g	271	12.7	60.6	77	1520	306	7.04

	SERVING QUANTITY	SERVING UNIT	CALORIES (kCal)	PROTEIN (g)	TOTAL CARBOHYDRATES (g)	SODIUM (mg)	POTASSIUM (mg)	PHOSPHORUS (mg)	TOTAL FAT (g)
SAGE									
ground	100	g	315	10.6	60.7	11	1070	91	12.8
1 Tbsp	2	g	6.3	0.21	1.21	0.22	21.4	1.82	0.256
CINNAMON									
ground	100	g	247	3.99	80.6	10	431	64	1.24
1 Tbsp	7.8	g	19.3	0.31	6.29	0.78	33.6	4.99	0.097
CUMIN									
seed	100	g	375	17.8	44.2	168	1790	499	22.3
1 Tbsp Whole	6	g	22.5	1.07	2.65	10.1	107	29.9	1.34
NUTMEG									
ground	100	g	525	5.84	49.3	16	350	213	36.3
1 tsp	7	g	36.8	0.41	3.45	1.12	24.5	14.9	2.54
CLOVES									
ground	100	g	274	5.97	65.5	277	1020	104	13
1tsp	6.5	g	17.8	0.39	4.26	18	66.3	6.76	0.845
PARSLEY									
fresh	100	g	36	2.97	6.33	56	554	58	0.79
dried	100	g	292	26.6	50.6	452	2680	436	5.48
CORIANDER									
seed	100	g	298	12.4	55	35	1270	409	17.8
leaves, raw	100	g	23	2.13	3.67	46	521	48	0.52
THYME									
fresh	100	g	101	5.56	24.4	9	609	106	1.68
dried	100	g	276	9.11	63.9	55	814	201	7.43
LEMON GRASS									
citronella, raw	100	g	99	1.82	25.3	6	723	101	0.49

	SERVING QUANTITY	SERVING UNIT	CALORIES (kcal)	PROTEIN (g)	TOTAL CARBOHYDRATES (g)	SODIUM (mg)	POTASSIUM (mg)	PHOSPHORUS (mg)	TOTAL FAT (g)
FENNEL									
Bulb, raw	100	g	31	1.24	7.3	52	414	50	0.2
seed	100	g	345	15.8	52.3	88	1690	487	14.9
1 Tbsp	5.8	g	20	0.92	3.03	5.1	98	28	0.864
DILL									
weed, fresh	100	g	43	3.46	7.02	61	738	66	1.12
weed, dried	100	g	253	20	55.8	208	3310	543	4.36
1 Tbsp	3.1	g	7.8	0.62	1.73	6.45	103	16.8	0.135
ANISE									
seed	100	g	337	17.6	50	16	1440	440	15.9
1 Tbsp	6.7	g	22.6	1.18	3.35	1.07	96.5	29.5	1.06
CARDAMOM									
spices	100	g	311	10.8	68.5	18	1120	229	6.7
1 Tbsp	5.8	g	18	0.63	3.97	1.04	65	10.3	0.389
CAYENNE									
pepper, red or cayenne	100	g	318	12	56.6	30	2010	293	17.3
1 tbsp	5.3	g	16.9	0.64	3	1.59	107	15.5	0.917
CURRY POWDER									
	100	g	325	14.3	55.8	52	1170	367	14
1 tbsp	6.3	g	20.5	0.90	3.52	3.28	73.7	23.1	0.882
PAPRIKA									
ground	100	g	282	14.1	54	68	2280	314	12.9
1 tbsp	6.8	g	19.2	0.96	3.67	4.62	155	21.4	0.877
CELERY									
celery, raw	100	g	14	0.69	2.97	80	260	24	0.17

	SERVING QUANTITY	SERVING UNIT	CALORIES (Kcal)	PROTEIN (g)	TOTAL CARBOHYDRATES (g)	SODIUM (mg)	POTASSIUM (mg)	PHOSPHORUS (mg)	TOTAL FAT (g)
SAFFRON									
	100	g	310	11.4	65.4	148	1720	252	5.85
1 tbsp	2.1	g	6.51	0.24	1.37	3.11	36.1	5.29	0.123
PEPPER, BLACK									
ground	100	g	251	10.4	64	20	1330	158	3.26
1 tbsp	6.9	g	17.3	0.72	4.42	1.38	91.8	10.9	0.225
PEPPER, WHITE									
ground	100	g	296	10.4	68.6	5	73	176	2.12
1 tbsp	7.1	g	21	0.74	4.87	0.355	5.18	12.5	0.151
TARRAGON									
dried	100	g	295	22.8	50.2	62	3020	313	7.24
1 Tbsp, leaves	1.8	g	5.31	0.41	0.904	1.12	54.4	5.63	0.13
1 Tbsp, ground	4.8	g	14.2	1.09	2.41	2.98	145	15	0.348
HORSERADISH									
	100	g	48	1.18	11.3	420	246	31	0.69
1 tbsp	15	g	7.2	0.18	1.7	63	36.9	4.65	0.103

Chapter 4
Foods to Avoid or Limit

Now that we have our extensive Food List when planning with your dietitian, you are now able to make informed choices about the ingredients that you will pick up on your next trip to the supermarket. But what foods do you really need to avoid or limit and how can you make sure that you can successfully align it with your kidney health goals?

High-Potassium Foods

What is potassium and why is it important to you?

Potassium is a mineral found in many of the foods you eat. It plays a role in keeping your heartbeat regular and your muscles working properly. It is the job of healthy kidneys to keep the right amount of potassium in your body. However, when your kidneys are not healthy, you often need to limit certain foods that can increase the potassium in your blood to a dangerous level.

Some medications are also known to increase potassium levels in the blood. If you have high blood pressure and are already prescribed with ACE Inhibitors or ARBs, or even water pills like spironolactone, you may need to keep your blood potassium levels always in check. You may experience weakness, numbness, and tingling if your potassium is at a high level. If it becomes dangerously too high, irregular heartbeat and heart attacks may occur.

How can you keep your potassium level from getting too high?

- You should limit foods that are high in potassium. Your renal dietitian will help you plan your diet so you are getting the right amount of potassium.
- Eat a variety of foods, but in moderation.

- If you want to include potatoes (a high potassium food) in your meal, you should peel, cut into small pieces, soak in water, boil and then drain them to remove some of their potassium.
- Do not drink or use the liquid from canned fruits and/or vegetables, or juices from meats.
- Remember that almost all foods have some potassium. The size of the serving is very important.
- Eating a large amount of low-potassium foods can turn it into a high-potassium meal.

What is a safe level of potassium in your blood?

Ask your doctor or dietitian about your recent blood potassium level and enter it here: _____

If it is 3. 5 – 5.0: You are in the SAFE zone
If it is 5.1 – 6. 0: You are in the CAUTION zone
If it is higher than 6.0: You are in the DANGER zone

High and Low Potassium Foods

Very High Potassium Avoid as much as you can	High Potassium Foos Consume Occasionally (not more than twice a week)	Low Potassium Foods
<ul><li>Banana</li><li>Orange juice</li><li>Prune juice</li><li>Coconut milk</li><li>Potato (white and sweet)</li><li>Tomato and products</li><li>Vegetable juice</li><li>Raisin bran cereal</li></ul>	<ul><li>Avocado</li><li>Cantaloupe,</li><li>honeydew melon</li><li>Dates, Dried fruits, prunes, raisins</li><li>Kiwi, Mango, orange,</li><li>Artichoke, broccoli, Brussels sprout</li></ul>	<ul><li>Apple, apple sauce, berries (strawberry, raspberries, blueberries), cherries, grapes, peaches, pear, pineapple, plum, Watermelon</li><li>Juices (cranberry,</li></ul>

• Salt substitute (Lite salt)	• Dried beans, lima beans • Mushroom (canned), • Winter squash and pumpkin • Spinach and most greens except kale • Organ meat • Chocolates	apple, grapes, and pineapple) • Asparagus, Cucumber, Eggplant • Bean sprouts, green beans, green peas • Cabbage, cauliflower, Kale, Lettuce • Celery, Onions, radish • Corn, rice • Noodle, pasta • Bread and bread products • Cereals except raisin bran • Cakes, cookies (without nuts and chocolates) • Coffee and tea

High potassium foods: food contains more than 200mg of potassium per serving.

- The portion size is ½ cup unless otherwise noted.
- Avoid very high potassium foods.
- You should not consume high-potassium foods more than twice per week or consume these foods together on same day.
- Meats, meat products, egg, fish, poultry, and cheeses are high in potassium; however, you should have these good protein sources in your diet because they are necessary to maintain good nutritional status.

Low potassium foods: foods contains less than 200mg of potassium per serving.

- A portion is ½ cup unless otherwise noted.
- You can eat the foods on the low potassium list daily but always keep the portion size in mind.
- Read Nutrition Label: If one serving contains more than 200mg of potassium, please find similar product with less potassium

High-Phosphorus Foods

What is Phosphorus?
Phosphorus is a mineral found in your bones. Along with calcium, phosphorus is needed for building healthy strong bones as well as keeping other parts of your body healthy.

Why is phosphorus important to you?
Normal working kidneys can remove extra phosphorus in your blood. When you have chronic kidney disease your kidneys cannot remove phosphorus very well. High phosphorus levels can cause damage to your body. Extra phosphorus causes body changes that pull calcium out of your bones, making them weak. High phosphorus and calcium levels also lead to dangerous calcium deposits in blood vessels, lungs, eyes, and heart. Phosphorus and calcium control is very important for your overall health.

What is a safe blood level of phosphorus?
A normal phosphorus level is 2.1 to 4.6 mg/dL. Ask your doctor or dietitian what your last phosphorus level was and write it here _____.

How can I control my phosphorus level?
You can keep your phosphorus level normal through diet and medications for phosphorus control. Your dietitian and doctor will help you. Below is a list of foods high in phosphorus.

High Phosphorus food to limit or avoid

Beverages	Ale, beer, chocolate drinks, cocoa, drinks made with milk, canned iced tea, dark colas
Dairy Products	Cheese, custard, milk, cream soups, cottage cheese, ice cream, pudding, yogurt
Protein	Beef liver, fish roe, oysters, crayfish, chicken liver, organ meats, sardines
Vegetables	Dried beans and peas: Baked beans, black beans, chickpeas, kidney beans, lima beans, lentils, northern beans, split peas, soybeans
Others	Bran cereals, brewer's yeast, caramels, nuts, seeds, wheat germ, whole grain products

What do I do if my phosphorus level is too high?

When your phosphorus level is too high, think about your diet and select foods from the low phosphorus list. Talk to your dietitian and doctor about making changes in your diet and ask about your phosphate binder prescription.

High Phosphorus Foods Instead of		Low Phosphorus Foods Try	
Food	**Phosphorus (mg)**	**Food**	**Phosphorus (mg)**
8 oz milk	230	8 oz non-dairy creamer or 4 oz milk	110 115
8 oz cream soup made with milk	275	8 oz cream soup made with water	90
1 oz hard cheese	145	1 oz cream cheese	30

½ cup ice cream	80	½ sorbet or 1 popsicle	0
½ cup lima or pinto beans	100	½ cup mixed vegetables of green beans	35
12 oz can cola	55	12 oz ginger ale or lemon soda	3
½ cup custard or pud-ding made with milk	150	½ cup pudding or custard made with non-dairy creamer	50
2 oz peanuts	200	1 ½ cup light or low fat popcorn	35
1 ½ oz chocolate bar	125	1 ½ oz hard candy, fruit flavors or jelly beans	3
2/3 cup oatmeal	130	2/3 cup cream of wheat or grits	40
½ cup bran cereal	140-260	½ cup non-bran cereal, shredded wheat, rice cereals or cornflakes	50-100

High-Sodium Foods

What is Sodium?

Sodium is a mineral found naturally in foods and it is the major part of table salt.

Why do I need to limit my sodium intake?

Some salt or sodium is needed for body water balance. However when you have high blood pressure, congestive heart failure or a kidney problem, you lose the ability to control sodium and water balance therefore you may experience the following:

- Thirst
- Fluid gain
- High blood pressure

By using less sodium in your diet, you can control these problems.

Hints to cut down sodium intake

- Cook with herbs and spices instead of salt
- Read food labels and choose foods low in sodium
- Avoid salt substitutes and especially low sodium foods made with salt substitutes because
- they are high in potassium. You should discuss with the dietitian if you have questions on salt substitutes.
- When eating out, ask for meat or fish without salt. Ask for gravy or sauce on the side:
  these may contain large amounts of salt and should be used in small amounts.
- Limit use of canned, processed and frozen foods.

Information about reading labels

- Sodium free - Only a trivial amount of sodium per serving
- Very low sodium - 35 mg or less per serving
- Low sodium - 140 mg or less per serving
- Reduced sodium - Foods in which the level of sodium is reduced by 25%
- Light or lite in sodium - Food in which the sodium is reduced by at least 50%
-

Rule of thumb: If salt is listed in the first five ingredients, the item is probably too high in sodium to use.

- All food labels have milligrams (mg) of sodium listed. Follow these steps when reading the sodium information on the label:

Know how much sodium you are allowed each day.

- Remember that there are 1000 mg in 1 gram. If your diet prescription is 2gm of sodium your limit is 2000 mg per day. Consider the sodium value of other food to be eaten during the day. New sodium recommendation is 2300mg (2.3g)per day.

Look at the package label.

- Check the serving size. Nutrition values are expressed per serving. If the sodium level is 500mg or more per serving, the item is not a good choice.

Compare labels of similar products.

- Select the lowest sodium level for the same serving size.

What kind of spices and herbs should I use instead of salt to add flavor?

- All spices, basil, bay leaf, caraway, cardamom, curry, dill, ginger, marjoram, rosemary, thyme, sage, tarragon and Mrs. Dash

Food	Avoid	Choose
Dairy	Buttermilk, Cottage cheese, regular cheese	2%, 1% or skim milk, low fat yogurt, low sodium cheese
Meats	**Processed and luncheon meats** Ham, bacon, salt pork, sausage Hotdogs, corned beef, Spam , Pastrami **Breaded or fried meats** Chicken, fish pork or beef **Canned meats in oil** Sardines, salmon, tuna	Fresh beef, veal, pork, poultry, fish, eggs Low-salt deli meat
Starches	Salted crackers or bread, Pretzels Potato chips, corn chips, tortilla chips, popcorn Instant mashed potatoes Mixed muffins, pancakes, potatoes, noodles, some dry cereals	Fresh bread, most commercial bread Unsalted chips, crackers, pretzels Read labels for dry cereals Unsalted popcorn
Vegetables	Canned vegetables Pickles, sauerkraut, olives, relish, vegetable juice, vegetable soup tomato products Frozen vegetables with cheese or cream sauces	All plain fresh and frozen vegetables Low-sodium canned vegetables Low-sodium tomato sauces Homemade or low-sodium soups
Fruits	None	All
Condiments	Table salt, garlic salt, celery salt Lite salt, Bouillon cubes, seasoning	Fresh garlic, fresh onion, garlic

124

	salt, onion salt, lemon pepper, meat tenderizer, flavored enhancers, salt substitutes, catsup/ketchup, mustard, salad dressing, soy sauce, steak sauce, barbecue sauce, teriyaki sauce, oyster sauce, hot sauce, Worcestershire sauce	powder, onion powder, black pepper, lemon juice, low-sodium or salt-free seasoning blends, vinegar, homemade or low sodium sauces and salad dressings, dry mustard
Others	**Convenience foods** TV dinners, Chili, spaghetti, frozen prepared foods, fast foods, canned raviolis, macaroni & cheese **Most Chinese, Mexican, and Pizza restaurants**	Low sodium frozen dinner, home-made casseroles without added salt, soups made with fresh or raw vegetables, fresh meat, rice, pasta or unsalted canned vegetables Request no salt on foods when eating out. Ask for sauces on the side when dinning out.

Understanding Nutrition Labels

I had to insert this topic on how to read and understand Nutrition Labels when you go grocery shopping. This would primarily help you with making Sodium in check, but potassium and protein details are also available for you to be able to make good choices about the items you pick-up at the supermarket.

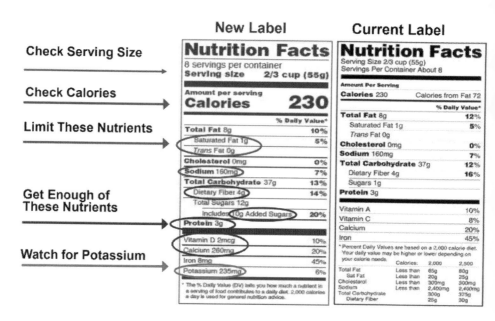

1. Portion Check: Make sure to look at the serving size and how many servings are in the container.

Example: one serving of this food = ⅔ cup. If I eat this whole package, I will eat about 5 cups.

2. Calorie Control: Calories tell us how much energy we get per serving.

Example: one serving of this food will give me 230 calories. If I eat the whole package, I will eat 1840 calories.
In General: Low = 50 Calories per serving; High = 400 Calories per serving

3. Limit These Nutrients:

Saturated Fat, Trans Fat, Sodium, and Added Sugars.
Low Fat = 3 g or less of total fat per serving
Low Sodium = 140 mg or less per serving; it is ok to choose less than 200 mg per serving

4. Get Enough of These Nutrients:

Look for foods higher in Fiber, Protein, and Vitamins and Minerals. These nutrients are important for health!

- Vitamin D, Calcium and Iron
- Dietary fiber lowers cholesterol and keeps you feeling full longer. Good Sources = 3 g or more per serving High Fiber = 5 g or more per serving
- Protein is important for keeping you energized, building and maintaining muscle mass, as well as wound healing.

However, please make sure to check with your doctor or dietitian on your individual daily requirements, especially Protein.

5. Watch for Potassium:

Based on your individual requirements, you may need to aim for low-potassium of less than 200 mg per serving. *Make sure to consult with your dietitian about your potassium requirement.*

Part II: Meal Planning and Recipes

Chapter 5
Meal Planning for
Kidney Health

Creating a Balanced Meal Plan

Creating a balanced meal plan for Chronic Kidney Disease (CKD) patients can be challenging due to the varying dietary requirements at each stage of the disease. However, it's crucial to remember that every patient is unique, and these guidelines should be tailored to individual needs and circumstances. Please consult with a healthcare provider or a renal dietitian before making any changes to your diet. In the next chapters, I have included carefully selected CKD recipes for you, but for now, here are general daily meal plan guidelines for each CKD stage:

Stage 1 and 2 Chronic Kidney Disease (CKD) Daily Meal Plan Guidelines

Patients with stage 1 and 2 chronic kidney disease (CKD) typically do not need to follow a specific renal diet. However, they should aim for a healthy, balanced diet that supports overall health and slows progression of the disease.

The dietary guidelines provided below are general in nature. Individual needs can vary greatly depending on age, sex, weight, physical activity level, and other health conditions. It's always important to consult with a healthcare provider or a registered dietitian for personalized advice.

Caloric Intake

A balanced caloric intake is crucial for maintaining a healthy weight. The daily caloric requirement varies based on individual factors, but here is a general guideline:

- For men: 2000 - 2500 calories/day
- For women: 1600 - 2000 calories/day

Proteins

Protein is essential for body growth, repair, and overall health. However, too much protein can put extra strain on kidneys. The recommended daily protein intake for CKD stage 1 and 2 is about:

- 0.8 grams of protein per kilogram of body weight.

Carbohydrates

Carbohydrates are the body's main source of energy. Choose complex carbohydrates like whole grains, fruits, and vegetables over simple sugars.

- Aim for about 45-65% of your daily calorie intake from carbohydrates.

Fats

Healthy fats are important for heart health. Opt for unsaturated fats found in fish, nuts and seeds, avocados, and olives.

- Aim for about 20-35% of your daily calorie intake from fats.

Sample Meal Plan

Here's a sample meal plan that fits within these guidelines:

Breakfast:
- 1 cup cooked oatmeal with a sprinkle of nuts
- 1 medium-sized banana
- 1 cup of skim milk or a dairy alternative

Lunch:
- 2 oz grilled chicken breast
- 1 cup steamed vegetables (like broccoli, cauliflower)
- 1/2 cup cooked brown rice

Afternoon Snack
- 1 small apple
- A handful of unsalted almonds

Dinner:
- 3 oz baked salmon
- 1 cup roasted sweet potato
- Side salad with mixed greens, tomatoes, cucumber, and a drizzle of olive oil dressing

Evening Snack:
- 1 cup low-fat yogurt with a sprinkle of berries

Remember to also stay hydrated and limit your sodium intake. Too much sodium can increase blood pressure and cause fluid retention, both of which can worsen kidney disease.

Also, note that as CKD progresses into later stages (3 to 5), dietary needs will change significantly, often requiring reduced intake of protein, potassium, phosphorus, and sodium. Regular monitoring and consultation with healthcare providers is crucial.

Stage 3-5 Chronic Kidney Disease (CKD) Daily Meal Plan Guidelines

As kidney function declines in the later stages of CKD (stages 3 to 5), the kidneys have a harder time removing waste products from protein metabolism, so protein intake often needs to be reduced. Likewise, potassium, phosphorus, and sodium levels need to be carefully monitored and limited, as the kidneys struggle to balance these minerals.

Remember, these meal plans are general guidelines. Individual needs can greatly vary. Always consult with a healthcare provider or a registered dietitian for personalized advice.

Stage 3 CKD Daily Nutrient Requirements

Caloric Intake:
- For men: 2000 - 2500 calories/day
- For women: 1600 - 2000 calories/day

Proteins:
- About 0.8 grams per kilogram of body weight.

Carbohydrates:
- Aim for about 45-65% of your daily calorie intake from carbohydrates.

Fats:
- Aim for about 20-35% of your daily calorie intake from fats.

Sodium:
- Aim for less than 2000 mg per day.

Potassium and Phosphorus:
- Your healthcare provider will advise you based on your blood levels.

Stage 3 CKD Sample Meal Plan

Breakfast:
- 1 cup of cream of wheat
- 1 slice of toast with 1 tablespoon of jelly
- 1 small apple
- 1 cup of coffee or tea

Lunch:
- Turkey sandwich: 2 oz turkey on whole grain bread with lettuce and mayonnaise
- 15 grapes
- Water or unsweetened iced tea

Afternoon Snack:
- 1 medium-sized peach
- A handful of rice cakes

Dinner:
- 3 oz grilled chicken breast
- 1 cup of cooked zucchini
- 1/2 cup of white rice
- Water or homemade lemonade (watching for sugar content)

Evening Snack:
- 1 cup of low-fat vanilla yogurt

Stage 4 CKD Daily Nutrient Requirements

Caloric Intake:

- For men: 2000 - 2500 calories/day
- For women: 1600 - 2000 calories/day

Proteins:

- About 0.6 grams per kilogram of body weight.

Carbohydrates:

- Aim for about 45-65% of your daily calorie intake from carbohydrates.

Fats:

- Aim for about 20-35% of your daily calorie intake from fats.

Sodium:

- Aim for less than 2000 mg per day.

Potassium and Phosphorus:

- Your healthcare provider will advise you based on your blood levels, but often the recommendation is to limit potassium to 2000-3000 mg per day and phosphorus to less than 800-1000 mg per day.

Stage 4 CKD Sample Meal Plan

Breakfast:
- 1/2 cup high-protein cereal with almond milk
- 1 slice toast with margarine
- Fresh blueberries (1/2 cup)
- Coffee or tea

Lunch:
- Tuna salad (made with low-sodium canned tuna) on a bed of lettuce
- Sliced cucumber and cherry tomatoes
- Apple sauce (1/2 cup)
- Water or unsweetened iced tea

Afternoon Snack:
- Rice cakes with a thin layer of cream cheese
- Fresh pineapple chunks (1/2 cup)

Dinner:
- 3 oz baked fish like cod
- Steamed green beans (1 cup)
- Mashed cauliflower (1/2 cup)
- Water or cranberry juice (unsweetened)

Evening Snack:
- Air-popped popcorn (2 cups)

Stage 5 CKD Daily Nutrient Requirements

(Not on Dialysis)

Caloric Intake:

- For men: 2000 - 2500 calories/day
- For women: 1600 - 2000 calories/day

Proteins:

- About 0.6 grams per kilogram of body weight.

Carbohydrates:

- Aim for about 45-65% of your daily calorie intake from carbohydrates.

Fats:

- Aim for about 20-35% of your daily calorie intake from fats.

Sodium:

- Aim for less than 2000 mg per day.

Potassium and Phosphorus:

- Your healthcare provider will advise you based on your blood levels, but often the recommendation is to limit potassium to 2000-3000 mg per day and phosphorus to less than 800-1000 mg per day.

Stage 5 CKD Sample Meal Plan

Breakfast:
- Cream of wheat (1/2 cup)
- White toast with jelly
- Sliced peaches (1/2 cup, canned in juice not syrup)
- Coffee or tea

Lunch:
- Egg salad sandwich: 1 boiled egg on white bread with lettuce and mayonnaise
- Apple slices
- Water or homemade lemonade (watching for sugar content)

Afternoon Snack:
- Rice cakes
- Fresh grapes (15)

Dinner:
- 2 oz roasted chicken
- Cooked carrots (1/2 cup)
- White rice (1/2 cup)
- Water or cranberry juice (unsweetened)

Evening Snack:
- Vanilla wafers (5)

These meal plans aim to restrict protein, potassium, phosphorus, and sodium intake while providing adequate calories and other nutrients. However, depending on the patient's specific lab results, dietary restrictions may be more or less strict. Remember, these are general guidelines and individual needs may vary greatly based on factors like age, sex, weight, physical activity level, and other health conditions. Always consult with a healthcare provider for personalized advice.

Portion Control and Serving Sizes

What distinguishes a portion from a serving?

A portion refers to the quantity of food you decide to consume in one sitting, whether it's at a restaurant, from a packaged product, or at your own dining table. On the other hand, a serving size is the specific amount of food defined on a product's Nutrition Facts label, or food label (as referred to on **Page 126**).

Serving sizes can vary across different products. These sizes can be quantified in various units such as cups, ounces, grams, pieces, slices, or even countable units like three crackers. Your chosen portion size may align with or differ from the listed serving size depending on how much you decide to eat.

To determine how many servings are in a container, check the top of the label where "Servings per container" is stated just above "Serving size." For instance, if a frozen lasagna lists 1 cup as the serving size and contains four servings per container, consuming 2 cups—or half the package—means you're eating two servings.

You'll need to do some simple calculations to understand how many calories and other nutrients you're actually consuming.

1 serving = 280 calories
2 servings = 280 × 2 = 560 calories

In this scenario, consuming two servings equates to doubling the calories—and other nutrients—listed on the food label. The serving size indicated on a food label may not necessarily reflect the appropriate amount for your dietary needs.

Hence, it's crucial to consult with your doctor and dietitian to determine your daily Protein, Sodium, Potassium, and Phosphorus requirements.

That's because how much of these nutrients you need each day to control your CKD may depend on:

- your age
- your current weight and height
- your metabolism
- whether you're male or female
- how active you are
- And most especially your lab numbers

As a CKD patient, you will need to always compare general guidelines with what your healthcare team prescribes. For the sake of having something tangible to compare to, I've made use of this "Handy" food portioning guide created by Covenant Home Care with my patients.

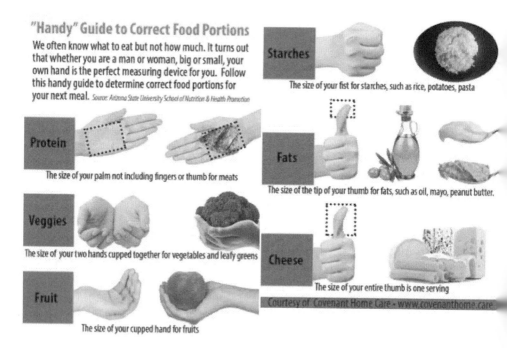

"Handy" Guide to Correct Food Portions

We often know what to eat but not how much. It turns out that whether you are a man or woman, big or small, your own hand is the perfect measuring device for you. Follow this handy guide to determine correct food portions for your next meal. *Source: Arizona State University School of Nutrition & Health Promotion*

Starches — The size of your fist for starches, such as rice, potatoes, pasta

Protein — The size of your palm not including fingers or thumb for meats

Fats — The size of the tip of your thumb for fats, such as oil, mayo, peanut butter.

Veggies — The size of your two hands cupped together for vegetables and leafy greens

Cheese — The size of your entire thumb is one serving

Fruit — The size of your cupped hand for fruits

Courtesy of Covenant Home Care - www.covenanthome.care

Tips For Grocery Shopping

The grocery store is your gateway to a diverse selection of food that can contribute to your wellbeing, especially when living with chronic kidney disease (CKD). Making smart choices here can greatly influence your health. Here are eight tips to help you navigate your grocery shopping experience.

Check The Quality Before Buying

Fresh and nutritious foods tend to last longer than their less healthy counterparts. Therefore, it's essential to examine fruits and vegetables for quality before purchasing. If they appear wilted or unusually discolored, consider opting out. Remember, seasonal produce often provides the best flavor and affordability.

Avoid Processed Foods

Grocery stores offer a mix of healthful and less healthful options. While processed foods may seem hard to dodge, there are strategies to help you steer clear. Begin by bypassing candy and sugary snacks, instead reaching for fresh fruits and vegetables. Also, be on the lookout for minimally processed alternatives, typically found nearer to natural food sections than boxed items or cereals.

Don't Shop on an Empty Stomach

Hunger can influence your shopping habits, leading you to purchase items you wouldn't usually eat due to reduced willpower. To avoid these potential pitfalls, try not to shop when you're feeling hungry or when your stomach is empty.

Write down a Grocery List and Stick with It!

Creating a detailed grocery list before setting foot in the store can help ensure that you only buy what you need. This strategy prevents impulse purchases of unhealthy items. Jot down your list on paper or use a digital note-taking app on your phone for convenience. And remember, with a meal plan, your shopping list is already prepared for you.

Buy Whole Foods

Whole foods—those in their most natural state without added artificial flavors, sweeteners, or preservatives—are the best choice. Studies indicate that individuals who consume more whole foods have a lower body mass index (BMI) and are less likely to develop heart disease and diabetes. As a general rule, avoid processed and packaged foods that contain unnecessary additives and fillers, which can add calories without contributing nutritional value.

Chapter 6
Renal Diet Recipes

Breakfast Recipes

Kidney-Friendly Smoothies

Green Detox Smoothie

Servings:	2	Preparation Time	10 minutes

INGREDIENTS	DIRECTIONS
1 cup Romaine lettuce 1 cucumber (chopped) 1/2 lemon (juiced) 1 pears (peeled and chopped) 1 tbsp ginger (grated) 1 tbsp ground flax seed 1 1/2 cups water 5 Ice cubes	1. Place all ingredients together in a blender. Blend until smooth. Be patient! No one likes clumps in their smoothies. It may take 1 minute or longer to get a great, smoothie-consistency. 2. Divide between glasses and enjoy!

NUTRIENT FACTS	TOTAL	PER SERVING
Calories (kCal):	164	82
Proteins (g):	4	2
Carbohydrates (g):	38	19
Fats (g):	2	1
Potassium (mg):	647	323.5
Phosphorus (mg):	100	50
Sodium (mg):	11.24	5.62

Fresh Mango Smoothie

Servings:	2	Preparation Time	10 minutes

INGREDIENTS	DIRECTIONS
1/2 cup frozen mango 1/2 cup frozen cauliflower 1 banana (medium) 1 1/2 cup water 1 1/2 tsp apple cider vinegar	1. Place all ingredients in your blender and blend until smooth. Pour into a glass and enjoy!

NUTRIENT FACTS	TOTAL	PER SERVING
Calories (kCal):	173	86.5
Proteins (g):	3	1.5
Carbohydrates (g):	43	21.5
Fats (g):	1	0.5
Potassium (mg):	648	324
Phosphorus (mg):	57	28.5
Sodium (mg):	17	8.5

Low-Potassium Breakfast Bowls

Breakfast Trail Mix

Servings:	3	Preparation Time	5 mins or less

INGREDIENTS	DIRECTIONS
1 cup Corn cereal 1 cup Rice cereal 1/2 cup Cocoa cereal 1/2 cup mini rice cakes (plain or apple cinnamon)	1. Mix all ingredients together in a medium bowl then divide into 1 cup portions. 2. Serve dry or with your preferred milk.

NUTRIENT FACTS	TOTAL	PER SERVING
Calories (kCal):	145	48.33
Proteins (g):	2	0.67
Carbohydrates (g):	32	10.67
Fats (g):	1	0.33
Potassium (mg):	210	70
Phosphorus (mg):	150	50
Sodium (mg):	600	200

Granola in Yogurt & Applesauce

Servings:	1	Preparation Time	5 mins

INGREDIENTS	DIRECTIONS
1/2 cup plain greek yogurt 1/4 cup unsweetened applesauce 1/4 cup granola 2 tbsps. pumpkin seeds	1. Mix the yogurt and apple sauce together in a bowl. 2. Top with granola and pumpkin seeds. Enjoy!

NUTRIENT FACTS	TOTAL	PER SERVING
Calories (kCal):	355	355
Proteins (g):	20	20
Carbohydrates (g):	31	31
Fats (g):	18	18
Potassium (mg):	336	336
Phosphorus (mg):	347	347
Sodium (mg):	196	196

Healthy Breakfast Sides

Guacamole Dip & Plantain Chips

Servings:	4	Preparation Time	10 mins

INGREDIENTS	DIRECTIONS
1 avocado (medium, ripe) 2 tbsps. nutritional yeast 1 tbsp lemon juice 1/4 tsp sea salt 1/2 cup plantain chips (store-bought or homemade)	1. In a bowl, mash together the avocado, nutritional yeast, lemon juice, and sea salt with a fork. 2. Place the guacamole in a bowl and serve with plantain chips. Enjoy!

NUTRIENT FACTS	TOTAL	PER SERVING
Calories (kCal):	247	61.75
Proteins (g):	7	1.75
Carbohydrates (g):	18	4.5
Fats (g):	18	4.5
Potassium (mg):	1470	367.5
Phosphorus (mg):	98	24.5
Sodium (mg):	611	152.75

Note:

1/2 cup plantain chips (store-bought or homemade): The content can vary greatly depending on the brand used. On average it might contain approximately 400mg of potassium, negligible amounts of phosphorus, and ~10-20mg of sodium.

Lunch Recipes

Light and Nourishing Salads

Farro and Chickpea Bowl

Servings:	3	Preparation Time	25 mins

INGREDIENTS

1 1/2 cup chickpeas (cooked)
2 tbsps. balsamic vinegar
1 tbsp maple syrup (to taste)
1/2 cup chives (chopped)
pinch of sea salt & black pepper (to taste)
1/2 cup farro (rinsed)
1/4 cup pesto
1 cup cherry tomatoes
1 tbsp avocado oil

DIRECTIONS

1. Combine the chickpeas, balsamic vinegar, maple syrup, chives, salt, and pepper in a bowl. Set aside.
2. Meanwhile, cook the farro according to the package directions.
3. Stir in the pesto. Set aside.
4. Toss the tomatoes in oil, salt, and pepper on a baking sheet.
5. Broil for six to eight minutes on the middle rack.
6. Divide the farro, chickpeas, and tomatoes evenly between bowls. Enjoy!

NUTRIENT FACTS

	TOTAL	PER SERVING
Calories (kCal):	415	138.33
Proteins (g):	15	5
Carbohydrates (g):	54	18
Fats (g):	16	5.33
Potassium (mg):	1090	363.33
Phosphorus (mg):	382	127.33
Sodium (mg):	512	170.67

Pasta Salad Niçoise

Servings:	6	Preparation Time	25 mins
		Chill Time	1-2 hrs

INGREDIENTS

4 cups cooked small shell macaroni
1 tablespoon olive oil
2 cups fresh green beans, cut in 1-inch pieces
1 /2 cup lemon juice
1 /3 cup olive oil
2 teaspoons dry mustard
1 tablespoon chopped fresh parsley
1 teaspoon basil
1 7-3/4-oz can tuna packed in water, drained
5 green onions, chopped, including tops
1 /4 teaspoon pepper

DIRECTIONS

1. Combine the chickpeas, balsamic vinegar, maple syrup, chives, salt, and pepper in a bowl. Set aside.
2. Meanwhile, cook the farro according to the package directions.
3. Stir in the pesto. Set aside.
4. Toss the tomatoes in oil, salt, and pepper on a baking sheet.
5. Broil for six to eight minutes on the middle rack.
6. Divide the farro, chickpeas, and tomatoes evenly between bowls. Enjoy!

NUTRIENT FACTS	TOTAL	PER SERVING
Calories (kCal):	304	50.67
Proteins (g):	15	2.50
Carbohydrates (g):	25	4.17
Fats (g):	16	2.67
Potassium (mg):	1545	257.50
Phosphorus (mg):	519	86.50
Sodium (mg):	381	63.50

Kidney-Friendly Sandwich/Wraps

Blueberry Coconut Crepes

Servings:	3	Preparation Time	15 mins

INGREDIENTS

1/4 cup canned coconut milk
1/4 cup frozen blueberries
4 eggs (large)
3 tbsps. coconut flour
1/8 tsp sea salt
2 tbsps. coconut oil (divided)

DIRECTIONS

1. Add the coconut milk, blueberries, eggs, coconut flour, and salt to a blender. Blend until smooth.
2. Heat a bit of the coconut oil in a skillet over medium heat.
3. Pour 1/4 cup of the batter at a time and gently swirl to spread it into a thin layer. Cook each side for about 30 seconds to one minute.
4. Repeat with the remaining batter and coconut oil.
5. Divide the crepes onto plates and enjoy!

NUTRIENT FACTS	TOTAL	PER SERVING
Calories (kCal):	248.01	82.67
Proteins (g):	9.99	3.33
Carbohydrates (g):	6.99	2.33
Fats (g):	20.01	6.67
Potassium (mg):	373.98	124.66
Phosphorus (mg):	567.99	189.33
Sodium (mg):	604.02	201.34

Stacked Vegetable Sandwich

Servings:	1	Preparation Time	5 mins

INGREDIENTS	DIRECTIONS
2 tbsps. hummus 2 slices whole grain bread 1/16 green lettuce (leaves separated) 1/4 tomato (medium, sliced) 1/4 cup radishes (trimmed, sliced) 1 tbsp red onion (sliced) 1/2 carrot (small, shredded)	1. Spread the hummus on the bread. 2. Add the remaining sandwich toppings. 3. Close the sandwich and enjoy!

NUTRIENT FACTS	TOTAL	PER SERVING
Calories (kCal):	317	317
Proteins (g):	14	14
Carbohydrates (g):	46	46
Fats (g):	9	9
Potassium (mg):	567	567
Phosphorus (mg):	177	177
Sodium (mg):	476	476

151

Dinner Recipes

Main Course

Couscous & Mushroom Bowl

Servings: 2	Preparation Time	25 mins

INGREDIENTS

2 eggs
2 tsps. extra virgin olive oil (divided)
1 cup Israeli couscous
2 cups water
2 tbsps. shallots (peeled, chopped)
2 garlic cloves (minced)
6 cremini mushrooms (sliced)
Pinch of sea salt & black pepper (to taste)

Note: Pinch = 1/16 teaspoon

DIRECTIONS

1. Place eggs in a saucepan and cover with water. Bring to a boil over high heat. Once boiling, turn off the heat but keep the saucepan on the hot burner. Cover and let sit for 10 to 12 minutes.
2. Strain the water and fill the saucepan with cold water. Once cooled, peel, halve and set aside.
3. Heat half the oil in a saucepan over medium heat. Add the couscous and toast for one to two minutes, stirring often.
4. Pour in the water and bring to a simmer and cook for 8 to 10 minutes, until cooked through. Drain excess water and set aside.
5. In a skillet over medium-low heat, pour in the remaining oil. Add the shallot and sauté until softened, about three minutes.
6. Then add the garlic and mushrooms and continue cooking until the mushrooms are cooked through and water is released, about five minutes.
7. Divide the couscous into bowls and top with mushrooms and the egg. Season with salt and pepper. Enjoy!

NUTRIENT FACTS	TOTAL	PER SERVING
Calories (kCal):	393	196.5
Proteins (g):	17	8.5
Carbohydrates (g):	59	29.5
Fats (g):	9	4.5
Potassium (mg):	530	265
Phosphorus (mg):	342	171
Sodium (mg):	304	152

Lemon, Garlic, & Herb Pasta

Servings:	3	Preparation Time	20 mins

INGREDIENTS

2 cups brown rice penne (uncooked)
2 cups chickpeas (cooked, drained)
1 tbsp extra virgin olive oil
1 1/2 tbsp lemon juice
2 garlic cloves (minced)
1/2 tsp oregano
pinch of sea salt & black pepper (to taste)
2 tbsps. parsley (chopped)
2 tbsps. basil leaves (chopped)
2 tbsps. fresh dill (chopped)

Note: Pinch = 1/16 teaspoon

DIRECTIONS

1. Cook pasta according to the package.
2. While the pasta is cooking, in a bowl, add the chickpeas, olive oil, lemon juice, garlic, oregano,
salt and pepper. Mix to combine and set aside to marinate.
3. Add the pasta to a serving bowl followed by the chickpea mix (including the liquid).
4. Toss to combine. Add the parsley, basil, dill and toss again. Divide into bowls and enjoy!

NUTRIENT FACTS	TOTAL	PER SERVING
Calories (kCal):	506	168.67
Proteins (g):	15	5
Carbohydrates (g):	89	29.67
Fats (g):	10	3.33
Potassium (mg):	1087	362.33
Phosphorus (mg):	622	207.33
Sodium (mg):	182	60.67

Note: You might want to reduce the following ingredients if you want to decrease the potassium and phosphorus content further:
2 cups brown rice contains approximately 308mg of potassium, 324mg of phosphorus,
2 cups chickpeas contain approximately 480mg of potassium, 270mg of phosphorus.

Side Dish

Halloumi Mushroom Tacos

Servings:	2	Preparation Time	20 mins

INGREDIENTS

1 tsp extra virgin olive oil
6 cremini mushrooms (sliced)
pinch of sea salt & black pepper
(to taste)
2.5 ozs halloumi (sliced)
1/2 cup pineapple (chopped)
2 tbsps. cilantro (chopped)
2 tbsps. lime juice
4 corn tortillas

Note: Pinch = 1/16 teaspoon

DIRECTIONS

1. Heat the oil in a pan over medium-high heat. Add the mushrooms and cook for three to five minutes or until golden brown. Season with salt and pepper. Remove and set them aside.
2. In a small bowl, mix together the pineapple, cilantro, and lime juice.
3. Divide the mushrooms and halloumi between the tortillas.
4. Top with pineapple salsa, season with additional salt and pepper if needed, and enjoy!
5. In the same pan, cook the halloumi slices until golden brown, about one to two minutes per side.

NUTRIENT FACTS	TOTAL	PER SERVING
Calories (kCal):	475	237.50
Proteins (g):	22	11
Carbohydrates (g):	36	18
Fats (g):	26	13
Potassium (mg):	604	302
Phosphorus (mg):	809	404.50
Sodium (mg):	905	452.5

155

Kidney-Friendly Dessert

Fresh Fruit and Sweet Cranberry Dip

Servings:	24	Preparation Time	10 mins
		Chill time	At least 30 mins

INGREDIENTS

8 ounces sour cream
1/2 cup whole berry cranberry sauce
1/4 teaspoon nutmeg
1/4 teaspoon ground ginger
4 medium pears, sliced into 12 slices each
4 medium apples, cut into 12 slices each
4 cups fresh pineapple, cut into bite-size pieces
1 teaspoon lemon juice

DIRECTIONS

1. Put sour cream, cranberry sauce, nutmeg and ground ginger in a food processor. It should be well-mixed, then transfer to a small bowl.
2. Then, cut the fresh fruit into small pieces. To prevent browning, toss apple and pear with lemon juice.
3. For final touches, arrange the fruits on platter with dip bowl then chill until ready.

NUTRIENT FACTS	TOTAL	PER SERVING
Calories (kCal):	70	2.92
Proteins (g):	0	0
Carbohydrates (g):	13	0.54
Fats (g):	2	0.08
Potassium (mg):	2791	116.29
Phosphorus (mg):	320	13.33
Sodium (mg):	129	5.38

Snacks and Beverages

Healthy Snack Options

Chocolate Peanut Butter Muffin

Servings:	9	Preparation Time	40 mins

INGREDIENTS

3 bananas (medium, ripe, mashed)
3 eggs
1/3 cup maple syrup
1/2 tsp vanilla extract
3 tbsps. Coconut oil
1/2 tsp sea salt
1 cup all natural peanut butter (divided)
1/2 tsp baking soda
1 tsp baking powder
1/2 cup cacao powder

DIRECTIONS

1. Preheat the oven to 375°F (190°C). Line a muffin tray with liners or use a silicone muffin tray.
2. Mix the mashed banana and egg together. Using a hand mixer or stand mixer is best, but a whisk will also work.
3. Slowly add the maple syrup and vanilla and continue mixing. Next, add the oil until an even consistency is achieved.
4. Add the salt and 3/4 of the peanut butter. Continue to mix, then add the baking soda and baking powder. Slowly add the cacao powder. Continue to mix until a pancake batter-like consistency is achieved.
5. Fill each muffin liner with the batter, approximately 1/3 cup each. Add the remaining peanut butter onto the top of each muffin and if desired, swirl with a toothpick.
6. Bake in the oven for 25 minutes or until muffin tops are firm. Remove from the oven, allow to cool in the muffin tin for 10 minutes before removing. Enjoy!

NUTRIENT FACTS	TOTAL	PER SERVING
Calories (kCal):	334	37.11
Proteins (g):	10	1.11
Carbohydrates (g):	26	2.89
Fats (g):	23	2.56
Potassium (mg):	3398	377.56
Phosphorus (mg):	860	95.56
Sodium (mg):	3002	333.67

Cheesy Tortilla Rollups

Servings:	4	Preparation Time	10 mins

INGREDIENTS

½ cup whipped cream cheese
2 flour tortillas, burrito size
½ cup raw spinach leaves, chopped
2 tablespoons onion, diced
2 tablespoons pimento, diced
½ cup crushed pineapple, drained
3 ounces unprocessed cooked
turkey breast, diced small
1 teaspoon Mrs. Dash® original
blend herb seasoning

DIRECTIONS

1. First, place cream cheese over each tortilla to cover and sprinkle with Mrs. Dash® herb seasoning.
2. In a bowl, put remaining ingredients and mix.
3. Divide mixed ingredients into 2 portions and place half on each tortillas.
4. Roll it up and slice each roll into 4 pieces.

NUTRIENT FACTS	TOTAL	PER SERVING
Calories (kCal):	956	239
Proteins (g):	41.3	10.33
Carbohydrates (g):	99.5	24.88
Fats (g):	45.67	11.42
Potassium (mg):	1080	270
Phosphorus (mg):	415	103.75
Sodium (mg):	916	229

Hydration Tips and Safe Beverages

Hydration is important for everyone, including those with chronic kidney disease (CKD). However, people with CKD may need to monitor and limit their fluid intake, especially as the disease progresses. Here are some hydration tips and safe beverage suggestions:

Monitor your Fluid Intake: Depending on the stage of your CKD and whether you're on dialysis, your healthcare provider or dietitian may recommend limiting your fluid intake. This includes not just drinks, but also foods that are liquid at room temperature like ice cream or gelatin.

Choose Water: Water is usually the best choice for hydration. It's calorie-free and doesn't contain sodium, potassium, or phosphorus.

Limit High-Potassium Drinks: Avoid beverages high in potassium such as orange juice, tomato juice, prune juice, and certain sports drinks.

Limit High-Phosphorus Drinks: Avoid drinks high in phosphorus like beer and cola drinks. Many dark-colored sodas contain phosphorus additives.

Limit Sodium-Rich Drinks: Be cautious with drinks like canned soups and broths, bottled sauces, sports drinks, and any beverages labeled as "high in sodium."

Limit Alcohol: Alcohol can dehydrate you and put more pressure on your kidneys.

Beware of Coffee and Tea: Both can be high in potassium. If you do drink coffee or tea, limit it to small amounts and count it towards your daily fluid allowance.

Avoid Energy Drinks: These often contain high levels of sodium, sugar, and caffeine.

Herbal Infusions: Some herbal teas might be a good option but be sure to check with your healthcare provider or dietitian first as some herbs can affect kidney function.

Stay Cool: Try to avoid getting too hot since sweating makes you lose more water.

Remember that these are general guidelines and individual needs can vary greatly. Always consult with your healthcare provider or dietitian to determine the best hydration plan for you.

Part III: Special Considerations

Chapter 7
Living with Kidney Disease

Myths and Facts about CKD

Despite having access to tons of information about kidney disease, it's still easier or rather more convenient to listen to what "he says-she says" about the disease, here are some common good-to-know myths and facts about CKD, so you can finally put to rest all the confusions and focus on what truly matters.

Myth 1: CKD is rare

Fact: CKD is not rare. It affects millions of people worldwide. According to the National Kidney Foundation, about 37 million American adults have CKD and most are unaware of it.

Myth 2: There are clear symptoms of CKD in the early stages.

Fact: Most people with early-stage CKD do not have clear symptoms. CKD is often called a "silent" disease because it can progress without noticeable signs. This underscores the importance of regular check-ups, especially for those with risk factors like diabetes, high blood pressure, or a family history of kidney disease.

Myth 3: If you have CKD, you will definitely need dialysis or a transplant.

Fact: Not everyone with CKD progresses to kidney failure requiring dialysis or a transplant. With appropriate management, including lifestyle changes and medications, the progression of CKD can often be slowed or halted.

Myth 4: A high-protein diet is good for your kidneys.

Fact: In fact, a high-protein diet can put strain on your kidneys and may accelerate kidney damage in those with CKD. A balanced diet that includes an appropriate amount of protein is recommended.

Myth 5: Drinking more water will keep your kidneys healthy and can cure CKD.

Fact: While staying hydrated is generally healthy, drinking more water than your body needs won't necessarily improve kidney function or cure CKD. In later stages of CKD, patients may actually need to limit fluid intake.

Myth 6: Only adults can get CKD.

Fact: While it's true that CKD is more common in adults, especially older adults, children can also develop kidney disease.

Myth 7: CKD only happens if you have a pre-existing health condition.

Fact: While conditions like diabetes and high blood pressure significantly increase the risk of developing CKD, it can also be caused by other factors such as certain medications, urinary tract obstructions, or inherited conditions.

Remember, if you have any questions or concerns about CKD, it's always best to consult with a healthcare provider for accurate information.

Coping strategies

Living with Chronic Kidney Disease (CKD) can be challenging, but there are several strategies that can help manage the condition and maintain a good quality of life.

Firstly, it's crucial to follow the treatment plan outlined by your healthcare team. This often includes managing underlying conditions like diabetes or hypertension, taking prescribed medications, following dietary guidelines, and maintaining a healthy lifestyle with regular exercise and smoking cessation if applicable.

Nutrition plays a key role in managing CKD. Working with a dietitian who specializes in kidney disease can be immensely helpful. They can provide personalized advice based on your specific needs and help you navigate dietary restrictions while ensuring you're getting the nutrients you need.

Regular check-ups are essential for monitoring kidney function and adjusting treatment as necessary. Regular blood tests can help track the progression of the disease and guide changes in medication or diet.

Managing emotional health is equally important. CKD can take a toll on mental well-being, leading to feelings of anxiety, depression, or fear. Mental health professionals such as psychologists or counselors can provide support and teach coping strategies.

Joining a support group can also be beneficial. Connecting with others who are going through similar experiences can provide comfort, reduce feelings of isolation, and allow for the sharing of practical advice. Organizations like the National Kidney Foundation (NKF) offer resources for finding local support groups.

Educating yourself about CKD is another important step. The more you understand about your condition, the better equipped you'll be to manage it. Reliable sources of information include your healthcare team and reputable health websites. The NKF and the American Kidney Fund offer extensive resources for patients and their families.

Lastly, don't hesitate to lean on your personal support network. Friends and family can provide emotional support, help with practical tasks, and accompany you to medical appointments. If you feel comfortable doing so, share your experiences with them so they can better understand what you're going through and how they can support you.

Living with CKD requires adjustments, but with the right resources and support, patients can lead fulfilling lives while managing their condition. Always remember, you are not alone in this journey, and there are numerous resources available to help.

Working with Your Healthcare Providers

Working effectively with your healthcare team is crucial in managing Chronic Kidney Disease (CKD). Here are some strategies to help you maximize this relationship:

1. Open Communication: Be open and honest with your healthcare providers. Share all your symptoms, even if you think they're not related to your kidney disease. The more information they have, the better they can tailor your treatment plan.

2. Prepare for Appointments: Before each appointment, make a list of any questions or concerns you have. This could include symptoms you've noticed, side effects from medications, or worries about diet and lifestyle changes.

3. Understand Your Treatment Plan: Make sure you fully understand your treatment plan and why each component is necessary. If something is unclear, don't hesitate to ask your doctor to explain it in simpler terms.

4. Role of the Dietitian: A dietitian specializing in kidney disease plays a crucial role in your healthcare team. They can provide personalized dietary advice based on your specific needs and help you navigate dietary restrictions while ensuring you're getting the nutrients you need. Regularly consult with your dietitian and update them on any changes in your health status.

5. Regular Monitoring: Regular blood tests and other diagnostic tests are essential for tracking the progression of CKD and adjusting treatment as necessary. Always attend scheduled appointments and follow through with recommended tests.

6. Follow Through: Adhere to the prescribed medication regimen and dietary advice, even when you're feeling well. Consistency is key in managing CKD.

7. Share Your Feelings: Don't forget to discuss your emotional health with your healthcare team. CKD can take a toll on mental well-being, leading to feelings of anxiety or depression. There are resources available to help manage these aspects of living with a chronic illness.

8. Involve Your Family: If comfortable for you, consider involving family members in discussions with your healthcare team. They can provide additional support, help remember information or instructions, and better understand what you're going through.

Remember, your healthcare team is there to support you in managing CKD. Don't hesitate to reach out to them with any concerns or questions you may have. They can provide valuable guidance and resources to help you navigate this journey.

Conclusion

Living with Chronic Kidney Disease (CKD) is a journey that requires strength, resilience, and most importantly, knowledge. This guide has been designed to provide you with comprehensive information and resources to help you manage your condition effectively. As we reach the end of this book, it's essential to revisit the key insights and takeaways that can empower you in your journey towards better kidney health.

Understanding CKD, its causes, diagnosis, and symptoms is the first step in managing this condition. Monitoring your kidney health regularly helps track your progress and make necessary adjustments to your treatment plan.

The cornerstone of managing CKD effectively lies in adhering to a kidney-friendly diet. This involves careful monitoring of key nutrients like potassium, phosphorus, sodium, and protein. Hydration and fluid management also play a crucial role in maintaining kidney health.

The renal diet food list provided in this guide serves as a valuable resource for making informed dietary choices. Remember, it's not just about avoiding certain foods but also about incorporating kidney-friendly foods into your diet.
Meal planning forms a significant part of managing your diet.

The importance of a well-researched food list cannot be overstated. It serves as a roadmap to navigate the often complex dietary needs associated with CKD. By understanding which foods are high in potassium, phosphorus, sodium, and protein, you can better control these key nutrients' intake, essential for managing your kidney health.

The guide'ines and sample meal plans provided for different stages of CKD offer a practical roadmap for creating balanced meals that cater to your nutritional needs without compromising on taste.

Portion control and understanding nutrition labels are essential skills that can help you manage your dietary intake more effectively. Grocery shopping tips offer practical advice on choosing the right foods during your shopping trips.

The recipe sections for breakfast, lunch, dinner, snacks, and beverages provide you with a variety of options to keep your meals interesting and enjoyable while still being kidney-friendly.

Living with CKD also involves dispelling myths and understanding the facts about the condition. Knowledge is empowering and can help you take control of your health.

Coping strategies and working effectively with your healthcare providers form an integral part of managing CKD. Open communication with your healthcare team can significantly enhance the effectiveness of your care.

In conclusion, while CKD may require certain lifestyle adjustments, having a well-researched food list at your disposal empowers you to take control of your health. Alongside regular consultations with your healthcare team and utilizing available resources, you can continue leading a fulfilling life. Remember, every step taken towards better management of your condition is a step towards improved health and well-being. You are not alone in this journey, and with the right knowledge and support, you can successfully manage CKD.

Appendix A: Glossary

Caloric Intake: The total amount of calories consumed in a day. Caloric intake can vary based on factors like age, sex, weight, and physical activity level.

Chronic Kidney Disease (CKD): A long-term condition where the kidneys do not work as well as normal. It is a progressive disease, which means it gets worse over time.

Dialysis: A treatment that filters and purifies the blood using a machine. This helps keep your body in balance when the kidneys can't perform these functions.

Dietitian: A healthcare professional who specializes in diet and nutrition. They can provide personalized dietary advice based on specific needs and health conditions.

Hypertension: Also known as high blood pressure, it's a condition that can damage the blood vessels and organs, including the kidneys.

Kidney Failure: A condition in which the kidneys lose their ability to function properly. It's also called end-stage renal disease (ESRD) when it reaches an advanced stage.

Phosphorus: A mineral found in many foods that the body needs for strong bones and teeth. In CKD, the kidneys can't remove excess phosphorus, leading to high levels in the blood.

Potassium: An essential nutrient that helps nerves and muscles communicate and also helps move nutrients into cells and waste products out of cells. In CKD, the kidneys may not be able to remove excess potassium from the blood.

Protein: A macronutrient that is essential for building muscle mass. It's commonly found in animal products, though some plants have protein as well.

Renal Dietitian: A dietitian who specializes in the dietary management of diseases that affect the kidney. They can provide personalized advice to patients with CKD.

Sodium: A mineral that's crucial for maintaining blood pressure, as well as for nerve and muscle function. In CKD, the body may struggle to balance sodium levels.

Trans Fat: A type of dietary fat that's associated with an increased risk of heart disease.

Unsaturated Fats: Healthy fats that are liquid at room temperature, such as olive oil and canola oil. They can help reduce levels of "bad" LDL cholesterol and increase "good" HDL cholesterol.

Urine: Liquid waste produced by the kidneys and excreted by the body. In CKD, the kidneys may not be able to produce urine effectively.

Albuminuria: A condition characterized by an excessive amount of the protein albumin in the urine, often indicating kidney damage.

Anemia: A condition marked by a deficiency of red blood cells or hemoglobin in the blood, leading to fatigue and weakness. It's common in people with CKD. Carbohydrates: One of the main types of nutrients, which are important sources of energy for the body.

Diabetes: A chronic disease that affects your body's ability to use sugar for energy. This can cause high blood sugar levels and damage many parts of the body, including the kidneys.

Dietary Fiber: Nutrient in our diet that is not digested by gastrointestinal enzymes but still fulfills an important role. It is also known as roughage or bulk.

Glomerular Filtration Rate (GFR): A test used to check how well the kidneys are working. Specifically, it estimates how much blood passes through the glomeruli each minute.

Hemodialysis: A treatment for kidney failure that uses a machine to send the patient's blood through a filter outside the body and return it back to the body.

Hyperkalemia: A higher than normal amount of potassium in the blood, often caused by decreased kidney function.

Hypokalemia: A lower than normal amount of potassium in the blood.

Nephrologist: A doctor who specializes in diagnosing and treating diseases of the kidneys.

Peritoneal Dialysis: A treatment for patients with severe chronic kidney disease where sterile fluid containing glucose is run into a patient's abdomen, absorbs waste products, and then drained out.

Proteinuria: The presence of excess proteins in the urine. In healthy persons, urine contains very little protein; an excess is suggestive of illness.

Renal: Pertaining to the kidneys.

Uremia: A high level of waste products in the blood due to poor kidney function or kidney failure.

Vitamins: Organic compounds required by the body in small amounts to sustain life. We need vitamins in our diets, because our bodies can't produce them fast enough to meet our daily needs.

Assessment: The act of making a judgment about something, often related to health and wellness.

Blood Levels: A term referring to the amount of a particular substance in the blood.

Body Weight: A person's mass or weight. Body weight is measured in kilograms, a measure of mass, throughout the world.

Calories: A unit used to measure the amount of energy that food provides when eaten and digested.

Carbohydrates: One of the three macronutrients, along with protein and fat. Our bodies use carbohydrates to make glucose, which gives us energy.

Dietary Guidelines: Recommendations given by reputed scientific organizations pertaining to health and nutrition.

Fats: One of the three main macronutrients, along with carbohydrate and protein. Fats are a concentrated source of energy.

Healthcare Provider: A person who helps prevent or treat illness or injury. This includes doctors, nurses, and allied health professionals.

Homemade: Made at home, rather than bought from a store or restaurant.

Kilogram: The basic unit of mass in the metric system.

Management: The process of dealing with or controlling things or people; in this context, it refers to managing one's health conditions.

Nutrient Requirements: The levels of intake of essential nutrients considered to be adequate to meet the known nutritional needs of practically all healthy people.

Physical Activity Level: A way to express a person's daily physical activity as a number, and is used to estimate a person's total energy expenditure.

Portion Control: Controlling the amount of food that one eats at one time, which can help control calorie intake.

Recommendation: An advised course of action provided by a healthcare professional.

Serving Size: The amount of a food or drink that is generally served. It is used to quantify recommended amounts, nutrient content and caloric values in dietary guidelines and food labels.

Unsweetened: Without added sugar or other sweet substances.

World Health Organization (WHO): A specialized agency of the United Nations responsible for international public health.

Appendix B: Resources

BIDMC Food Prioritization Project by https://www.renaltracker.com
Food List Reference: USDA FoodData Central – https://www.fdc.nal.usda.gov
The Basics of a Kidney-Friendly Diet:
1. National Kidney Foundation. (2015). A to Z Health Guide. https://www.kidney.org/atoz/content/diet
2. Kidney Care UK. (2021). Fluid control for kidney patients. https://www.kidneycareuk.org/about-kidney-health/living-kidney-disease/kidney-kitchen/factsheets/fluid-control-kidney-patients/
3. National Institute of Diabetes and Digestive and Kidney Diseases. (2017). Eating & Nutrition for Hemodialysis. https://www.niddk.nih.gov/health-information/kidney-disease/kidney-failure/hemodialysis/eating-nutrition

Meal Planning for Kidney Health
1. National Kidney Foundation: Nutrition and Chronic Kidney Disease (Stages 1–4) https://www.kidney.org/atoz/content/nutrichronic
2. National Kidney Foundation: Nutrition and Early Kidney Disease (Stages 1–4) https://www.kidney.org/sites/default/files/11-50-0113_patbro_nutrition.pdf
3. National Kidney Foundation: Potassium and Your CKD Diet https://www.kidney.org/atoz/content/potassium
4. National Kidney Foundation: Phosphorus and Your CKD Diet https://www.kidney.org/atoz/content/phosphorus
5. American Dietetic Association: Chronic Kidney Disease (CKD) and Diet: Assessment, Management, and Treatment https://www.eatrightpro.org/-/media/eatrightpro-files/practice/position-and-practice-papers/position-papers/kidneydisease.pdf
6. World Health Organization: Protein and Amino Acid Requirements in Human Nutrition https://www.who.int/nutrition/publications/nutrientrequirements/WHO_TRS_935/en/
7. Dietary Guidelines for Americans https://www.dietaryguidelines.gov/sites/default/files/2019-05/2015-2020_Dietary_Guidelines.pdf

Portion Control and Serving Sizes
1. https://www.niddk.nih.gov/health-information/weight-management/just-enough-food-portions
2. Food Portioning: www.covenanthome.care

Myths and Facts about CKD
1. National Kidney Foundation: 10 Common Myths About Chronic Kidney Disease
   https://www.kidney.org/news/ekidney/march_2013/myths
2. American Kidney Fund: Kidney disease facts
   https://www.kidneyfund.org/kidney-disease/kidney-disease-facts/
3. National Institute of Diabetes and Digestive and Kidney Diseases: Eating & Nutrition for Hemodialysis
   https://www.niddk.nih.gov/health-information/kidney-disease/kidney-failure/hemodialysis/eating-nutrition
4. Mayo Clinic: Chronic kidney disease
   https://www.mayoclinic.org/diseases-conditions/chronic-kidney-disease/symptoms-causes/syc-20354521

Appendix C: Index

A Note from the Author

As this book draws to a close, I trust it has become a reliable companion, always at hand as you grapple with the daily challenges of CKD dieting.

For every individual wrestling with kidney disease, my heartfelt desire is for you to triumph over this struggle through informed choices and self-management.

Thank you for selecting this book. While our personal interactions may be limited, know that your support holds immense value for me and is deeply appreciated.

If this book has been instrumental in aiding your journey, I invite you to express your thoughts through an Amazon review. This can be done either by scanning the QR code or typing the link into your web browser.

https://go.renaltracker.com/book2review

Again, thank you so much for your support and see you soon!

Sincerely,

Janeth Kingston, BSN RN

Made in the USA
Middletown, DE
28 August 2024